THE WONDER OF
BRIAN COX

THE WONDER OF
BRIAN COX

THE UNAUTHORISED BIOGRAPHY OF THE MAN
WHO BROUGHT SCIENCE TO THE NATION

BEN FALK

JOHN BLAKE

Published by John Blake Publishing Ltd,
3 Bramber Court, 2 Bramber Road,
London W14 9PB, England

www.johnblakepublishing.co.uk

www.facebook.com/Johnblakepub facebook
twitter.com/johnblakepub twitter

First published in hardback in 2012

ISBN: 978-1-84358-953-2

British Library Cataloguing-in-Publication Data:

A catalogue record for this book is available from the British Library.

Design by www.envydesign.co.uk
Printed in Great Britain by CPI Group (UK) Ltd

1 3 5 7 9 10 8 6 4 2

Papers used by John Blake Publishing are natural, recyclable products made from
wood grown in sustainable forests. The manufacturing processes conform to the
environmental regulations of the country of origin.

Every attempt has been made to contact the relevant copyright-holders, but some
were unobtainable. We would be grateful if the appropriate people could contact us.

For Laura

CONTENTS

ACKNOWLEDGEMENTS

As ever with a book of this kind, there are dozens of people to thank: Christina – I couldn't do it without you, thanks for letting me be a grump when I need to be; Mum and Dad, for watching his shows even if you didn't understand them; John Blake and Allie Collins for asking in the first place and for their guidance; and all my other friends, who chivvied me along and didn't look too bored when I espoused a fact I'd learned. For lending help and providing material: Mick Taylor, you're a legend; Colin Paterson and Elizabeth Alker, my northern correspondents; Anwar Brett, appreciate the delve into the archives and Tim Haughton, thanks for your superlative memory. Gregg LaGambina and Tasha Robinson from The A.V. Club, Andrew N. Holding from Skeptics in the Pub, Cambridge, Catherine Gerbrands and *The Stage* newspaper, Darren Rea from sci-fi-online.com, Brian Clegg of Popularscience.co.uk, Universetoday.com and Nancy Atkinson, the Press Association and Roger Crow – you all rule. And last, but not least, the incredible people who either let me talk to them or pointed me in the right direction: Amanda Groom, who went above and beyond; Professor John Dainton, Professor Paddy Regan, Imran Khan, Tony Steel, Ali Paterson, Joey Tempest, Sara Webb, Julie Dawn Cole, Alan Franks, Ian Willetts, Victoria Asare-Archer, Claire Bithell, Petri Lunden, Jude Rogers, John McKie, Andy Welch and Alex Hardy – you made this a story worth telling. Nikki Kennedy, I love your legal mind, and thanks to the dim sum place opposite Manchester University for sheltering me from the rain. And finally a big thank you to Gia Milinovich and Professor Brian Cox – interesting, intelligent people who will no doubt write their own stories one day. I hope this may at least act as a memory-jogger.

INTRODUCTION

There's not an arm-patch in sight. Instead, a young-looking man with a mop of black hair settles comfortably in a chair on the stage of the Royal Festival Hall in London, bespectacled colleague to his left. He's wearing a grey T-shirt, black jacket and trainers – the trousers, of course, black. The whoops die down. That's right, there was whooping when these two men in their early forties walked casually onto the stage in front of 2,500 paying spectators, who had come to hear them talk about quantum physics. It's an eclectic crowd – young, old, male, female – not the fusty audience you might expect for what amounts to a discussion about two-slit theory and how it's possible for a particle to skip to any part of the universe in a heartbeat. Personally, I struggle to understand what they're talking about, but then I gladly gave up science at GCSE. It's not that I don't appreciate the subject, it's simply my brain is not equipped to deal with these kinds of concepts.

Professor Brian Cox, for it is he beneath the floppy black fringe (though thin strips of grey are beginning to poke through), believes anyone can understand the basics of quantum mechanics with a bit of application and over the next 45 minutes, he and his colleague, Professor Jeff Forshaw, try to do just that. It probably works for some people; it doesn't for me. But whether they understand it or not, the packed house is on the edge of their seats. When Cox opens up the floor to Q&A after their lecture, hands shoot up so quickly and strenuously they are practically wrenched out of their sockets. For the most part, he answers the questions patiently, stopping to rant about how angry he gets when scientists are equated to an interest group, to make fun of the way he sometimes speaks on television and occasionally gives short shrift to someone, like the man who earnestly enquires about a true vacuum and whether it's possible to create one. The answer, says Cox, is no. Though one person does request tips on seeing the Northern Lights, no one asks if they can marry him, or have his babies, or have him sign their breasts – at least not out loud. But as he stands in his familiar way, legs fairly wide apart as he clarifies a point on a large teacher's notepad, it's clear that Professor Brian Cox is without doubt the most famous and celebrated scientist in Great Britain right now and possibly of the last 10 years.

The funny thing is, it's not because of something he's discovered, or because of the Nobel Prize he won. Instead, Cox – labelled jokily by his friends as the 'Peter Andre of particle physics' – has become as famous as he is because of his ability to communicate science. His 2010 BBC series *Wonders of the Solar System* averaged a staggering 5 million viewers a week, while the 2011 follow-up, *Wonders of the Universe*, did even better, with an audience of 6 million viewers a week. Because of this, he's mentioned in the same breath as Sir Patrick Moore, or Sir David Attenborough – science presenters who have captured the zeitgeist. A particle physicist by trade, Cox is also a professor at Manchester University, where he completed his doctorate, as well as a Royal Society University Research Fellow. He has worked on the H1 project at HERA accelerator in Hamburg, a predecessor to his current official job as a researcher on the ATLAS experiment at the Large Hadron Collider at the European Organisation for Nuclear Research (CERN) in Geneva, Switzerland. And he has also published a number of successful academic papers in addition to four books. In other words, he really knows his stuff.

Yet there's another reason why Cox is so comfortable on stage at the Royal Festival Hall. His past life includes stints in the chart-topping band D:Ream, as well as the rock band Dare, playing keyboards on tours around the world and on BBC's *Top of the Pops*. David Attenborough can't say he was in the band at the Labour Party election victory bash of 1997. Nor can Patrick Moore lay claim to being one of *People* magazine's Sexiest Men Alive, a poll in which Cox was included in 2009. Furthermore, he's universally considered a nice guy. If you're looking for tales of drug abuse, broken hearts and plates thrown at assistants, you won't find them here. Try as I might – and for the sake of balance I *did* try – I couldn't find anyone who questioned his integrity or personality, though some took issue with his screen presence, while others showed disgruntlement at his ubiquity.

All this and more will be examined here, including several exclusive interviews with those who knew Cox as a student at Oldham Hulme Grammar School, a post-graduate student in Germany, a big-haired rocker behind the keys onstage at Maple Squash Club in Oldham and beyond. Although he hasn't participated in this book, there are exclusive, never-before-seen quotes from the man himself. I interviewed him just before he became really famous in February 2010 when he was starting to promote *Wonders of the Solar System*. According to my emails, he was very difficult to pin down, his insanely busy schedule and desire to do it all already proving tricky to manage. I finally managed to contact him at his house in Battersea, where via an occasionally poor phone line (not sure why when it was just across the river in London, shouldn't he be able to fix it?), he talked with passion about his programmes and future plans.

Though I knew little about him, I was already intrigued as to how someone who has been hired as a professional scientist rather than a professional presenter finds time to ensure he maintains his academic credentials and whether he senses resentment from within his own community. 'I'm fairly sure it's accepted now that someone needs to [do these sorts of programmes],' he told me. 'We're always having funding crises one way or another and we're always fighting for public and governmental support. It's changed over the last 10 years and it's widely accepted that some people have to do it. As long as you have a small number, it works.' Still, he continued: 'I think the reason you're valued on TV or writing articles is because you're a scientist and have a particular way of looking at the world, or an attitude that comes from being a research scientist. I think if you lose it, you become less good at presenting it.'

More than two years on and a whole load of fame later, it's interesting to wonder whether he sticks by that edict. One former boss revealed to me that following the first series of *Wonders...* he bumped into Cox at a party, where the Professor told him that he was returning to science. Other fellow scientists suggest maybe his greatest achievement will be his ability as a communicator. There's no doubt Cox has used his fame, such as it is, for the good, whether visiting schools and encouraging pupils to pursue physics, or arguing with relevant government ministers for better funding for science. Indeed the so-called 'Brian Cox Effect' which will be examined in more detail later has been bandied about by the media, who argue more kids have taken up science as a result of his documentaries.

Cox's great hero, the American writer and scientist Carl Sagan, wrote in his book *Cosmos* of his belief of man's inherent desire to understand the building blocks of our world, our connection to the universe and how this would best be communicated through the language of television. Sagan's similarly-titled TV series was three years in the making and its estimated audience was ultimately 140 million. In his 1980 text to accompany the landmark show, he wrote: 'Whatever road we take, our fate is indissolubly bound up with science. It is a matter of simple survival for us to understand science.' As Cox himself told me: 'Someone's got to do the actual science or you'd have nothing to talk about.' But as CERN continues to learn more and more about the fabric of our universe and neutrinos fly around the world at speeds we cannot possibly fathom, perhaps it's down to Professor Brian Cox to tell us all about it. And if he happens to have been part of a band who had a No. 1 hit, then hey, why not?

One thing should be pointed out here. Obviously, the publishing industry cannot predict the speed of scientific progress. As such, all science facts contained herein are correct up to the end of January 2012. If aliens show up or someone decides to go back to the future after that, please forgive me for not mentioning it within these pages.

CHAPTER 1

CHILDHOOD

Most of what you need to know about why Brian Cox turned out the way he did comes from the day he turned 10 years old. It was 1978 and most children celebrating their tenth year would have asked for a Han Solo action figure. Not the future Professor Cox, though: he requested a fuse box. 'It was a four-way fuse box,' he explained. 'And the reason is, I had a shed at my granddad's house with a friend of mine, who I'm still very good friends with, that we used to wire up. We had a railway transformer in his garage and ran 12 volts into this shed, and put switches in it and lights, and just sat there.' It's safe to say Brian Cox knew what he wanted to do from an early age. So, it seems, did his friend – he now works for the electricity board in Manchester.

Brian Edward Cox was born to David and Barbara Cox (née

Holden) on 3 March 1968 at the Oldham and District General Hospital, as it was then known. Just off the Rochdale Road, it is now best known for being the birthplace of Louise Brown, the world's first 'test-tube' baby, 10 years later. Cox was taken home to Oakbank Avenue in the suburb of Chadderton, where the family lived in a semi-detached house. A quaint, quiet area outside the more brutish metropolises of Manchester and Oldham, it has a small shopping area in its heart, while the environs are filled with houses that get increasingly prettier the further away from the centre you go (as well as further up the small hills). He grew up in a space-obsessed household – his father still has a newspaper cover from the moon landing in July 1969 on the wall of his home. On Christmas Eve 1968, Cox sat on his father's knee to watch *Apollo 8* go round the back of the moon. This same launch has become his own son George's favourite. 'When we watch it on YouTube, someone shouts "clear the tower!" really loudly,' he says. Now whenever George wants to see *Apollo 8* on its way, he shouts the same thing.

'It was always on in the house,' said Cox of footage from various space missions. 'I don't remember watching it, but I remember growing up in a house that had pictures of the moon landings on the walls.' Indeed, his father made sure his son watched Neil Armstrong and his team walk on the moon for the first time in 1969. 'I was one year old and I watched them!' Cox recalled. Space and man's exploration into it had a profound effect on the future scientist. 'I was always fascinated by space exploration,' he has said. 'I think it was really that that triggered my interest in science and I found that I always thought of myself as a scientist. I wanted to do something. I didn't necessarily want to be an astronaut, but I wanted to be involved – so I just latched on to everything else. My interest in science grew, but I think that was the beginning.'

Later on, as a pre-pubescent schoolboy, he was entranced by one of the greatest television series ever made about science. Cox fans – and more specifically, those who love *Wonders of the Solar System/Universe* – would do well to seek out Carl Sagan's landmark show *Cosmos* (and the accompanying book) to see what was intended to be its 21st-century equivalent. Sagan approached science not just as an academic, but as a poet, too. It's not hard to see the parallels. Certainly it only added to a young Brian Cox's desire to pursue science. 'For me, television played a key role in making me a scientist and that's partly down to the quality of the science programming when I was growing up,' he revealed. 'For me, the greatest of them all was Carl Sagan's *Cosmos* – 13 hours of lyrically, emotionally engaging accurate and polemical broadcasting.' It wasn't only imported TV that piqued his interest, though. Patrick Moore's *The Sky at Night*, which debuted on the BBC in 1957, became a soundtrack to Cox's life. He has said Moore is the reason why he became a professional scientist. And despite all his success, one of his greatest achievements was joining the 88-year-old, monocled Moore for the show's 700th edition in 2011. 'He was my total hero,' said Cox. 'I took along a little book I won at school in 1978, Moore's *Book of Astronomy*, and got him to sign it while I was there. That meant a lot to me.'

By the time he was 6 years old, he was collecting astronomy cards and sticking them in an album. He loved a children's book called *The Race Into Space* (he is even seen flicking through it on-screen during one of his later TV shows), but what got him excited then is a letdown now. 'That's a disappointing book when you look at it now!' he said. 'It says we were going to be on Mars by 1983.' Unsurprisingly, by the age of 8, he had already received his first telescope. 'I was a very, very, very nerdy child,' he told the *Daily Mail*. He would peer up at the Oldham sky, using his star maps as a guide. 'For as long as I can remember,' he said, 'that's what I wanted to do.'

But if the astronomy thing didn't work out, there was another pursuit occupying much of his time. Bus-spotting was a serious business for Cox. Along with a friend, he kept a book filled with all the registration numbers from the vehicles of Greater Manchester Transport. Whenever he had the chance, he went to Oldham and ticked off the ones he saw. Sometimes they went into Manchester. He was a particular fan of the number 51, noting its nice bodywork and large pneumatic gears. 'I like machines,' he says. Bus-spotting parlayed into plane-spotting. On a weekend, he would head to Manchester Airport to see the departing and arriving flights in all their close-up glory. 'I didn't go out of the country until I was 17,' he later revealed, 'so it was a really romantic thing to see all these planes flying in from all over the world.'

By this time, he had a younger sister called Sandra. Despite growing up in the same house as machine-lovers and space nuts, she chose not to follow the same path as her brother and eventually became a partner at accountants KPMG in Manchester. She married a work colleague and has two children of her own. Life in the Cox household was a fairly typical story for a middle-class Northern family in the Seventies. Christmas was spent round the telly. 'I liked growing up with Christmas,' Cox told the *Guardian*. 'I liked watching Morecambe & Wise, I like the Queen's speech because it was on and everyone listened to it. It's a specifically Seventies Christmas that I like. I like Christmas *Top of the Pops* with Shakin' Stevens on it.'

Both parents worked in banks – Lloyds and Yorkshire banks in Oldham – his father as a manager and his mother a teller. Because they were away during the day, Cox spent much of his time at his grandparents' house. When he reached school age, he was there most lunch times. He remembers listening to Frank Sinatra's 'Come Fly With Me' on a large wooden radiogram with BBC Light Service embossed on the wood. 'I suppose like most people growing up, my dad and my granddad had records and this was one of the ones I remember,' he said. 'Big cover of Sinatra on the front, with this remarkable pose – it was one of the first things I latched onto, one of the first pieces I listened to.'

Both his grandparents started off by sweeping the floors of the Oldham cotton mills, but his grandfather was a remarkable man. Born in 1900, Cox senior left school in 1914 and worked his way up the corporate ladder at the company to run it. Ironically, despite no formal training, he ended his working life as a scientist of sorts. 'My granddad did write a couple of academic papers,' Cox remembered to Radio 4. 'He became a chemist and ran a dying company – he came up with a process of dying nylon black.' Though Grandpa Cox hadn't completed his schooling, he was keen to make sure his son didn't suffer the same fate. 'My dad was the first person to do A-levels and he went to a grammar school,' said Cox. 'My granddad and grandma both worked in cotton mills. I was the first person in my family to go to university.' He described it as an inspirational 20th-century story – each successive generation getting more and more opportunities. 'I think it's a progression that I fear and I hear is less possible now,' he remarked. 'Which would be a disaster.'

Cox's first school was Chadderton Hall, a good primary and literally adjacent to his house. The family home was next door to the playing fields for the school and though he wasn't supposed to, he used to climb over the fence to get there in the mornings and after lunch. Cox always enjoyed his schooling, even then academia appealed. However, he did have something he wanted to raise with those who had created the curriculum. 'One thing I wasn't happy about at junior school was that I wanted to have physics lessons but you didn't get specific science lessons until you were senior school,' he explained. 'My interest in physics and astronomy came from outside school.' Nevertheless, he indulged his geeky interests in other ways. 'Believe it or not, the head at my junior school was called Mr Perfect,' he told *The Times*. 'He was brilliant. He ran after-school classes in maths and English, and let kids stay on to play board games. When we played Risk, we would discuss each move and only make one or two moves a week, so one game would go on all term.'

Cox looks back with fondness on what he got up to as a child, inevitably turning to a scientific reference, albeit a science fiction one, to illustrate his point. 'As a geek, I like *Star Trek*,' he told *Discovery.com*. 'There's a very famous *Star Trek* episode where Captain Picard goes back in time and he gets the opportunity to tell himself as a teenager how he should behave, don't make these mistakes that you made, don't get in this car and crash it, and then he goes back to real life and he's not a captain anymore, he's just some useless guy who cleans the bathroom on the *Enterprise*. And that's a really vital lesson, I think: you are what you are and if you like where you've got to, then you don't know which little bits of behaviour when you were a kid got you there. So I wouldn't change anything, because I'm quite happy with where I've got to. Even though I did some silly things, maybe they're the things that allowed me not to do them in the future.'

CHAPTER 2

SCHOOL

At the age of 11, it was time to go to senior school. Just three miles or so away from Chadderton, just off Chamber Road, south of Oldham was Oldham Hulme Grammar School – a private school, which was divided in two for boys and girls. A giant wooden door ostensibly separated the two sexes. Though both of Cox's parents had good jobs, it was still something of a struggle to pay the fees. 'They couldn't afford it, really – I think my grandparents chipped in,' he told the *Guardian*. 'I don't know how expensive it was relative to wages, but it was a huge thing for them to do that. But it was a great source of pride, I think, that my dad had passed the 11+ and gone to grammar school and got A-levels. And I think he wanted me to go to grammar school, basically – if it had been free. It's a classic 20th-century story, but when you read, now, that that kind of route has been closed off for people, that we're less socially mobile than we ever were, it's tragic.'

Though the fabric of the school has been around since 1611, the Oldham Hulme Grammar School opened on its current site in 1895. Hidden down College Lane, it is set in a suburban area, austere but welcoming. The buildings sit atop a hill, looking out over a factory chimney, which extends from the valley below. A long driveway weaves its way through to the main reception, a small football pitch in front, the library block outside. Varnished brown panelling lines the walls and a poster of Oldham the dog – given to Robert Scott for his last, doomed expedition to the South Pole in 1910 – is nailed proudly to a pillar in the main hall. It feels academically stimulating, buzzy – the kind of place where ex-pupils return as teachers. Television actress Sarah Lancaster attended the girls' school (and actually overlapped with Cox by a couple of years); journalist and presenter John Stapleton graduated from there in the early 1960s. Described by Cox as 'a traditional boys' school', alumni speak with enthusiasm of English masters who wore their university gowns and were nicknamed 'Batman' and terrifying chemistry teachers. 'It was a very good school, but quite old-fashioned,' says Tim Haughton, an old school friend of Cox. 'There were some very unusual characters, teacher-wise – very out of the mould of those old films, the strange professor. People who wouldn't have fitted into a private school setting, but wouldn't have fitted in at a comprehensive either.'

The boy's uniform was typical: a black blazer with school badge, white shirt, dark trousers, grey socks and black shoes (the tie depended on the house you were in). Echoing public school, boys were divided into different 'houses' as a means of encouraging competition and for ease of classroom streaming. It was just one of the ways that the former grammar school showed off its private school status. 'The kids were generally middle-class,' Haughton adds, 'although there were people on assisted places but generally a well-to-do background.' While in 1979 not everyone went on to the sixth form and university, Oldham Hulme had a good scholastic reputation and fostered curricular and extra-curricular development. Nowadays, the music rooms are inundated with synthesisers, but this wasn't the case in the early 1980s. The physics labs – where Cox spent much of his time – were crowded with scientific experiments, Bunsen burners and oscilloscopes; the desks arranged in a horseshoe shape in front of where the teacher stood.

When Cox arrived at the school he was already focused on pursuing science – he hadn't had the opportunity at Chadderton Hall and was itching to go once he hit senior school. 'Initially, you were split in classes by your house,' remembers Haughton. 'It was only when you got to 13, 14, that the classes got much more integrated – you could opt into certain lesion and opt out of them.' Determined to concentrate on the scientific disciplines, Cox quickly saw no need for French and dropped the subject, something he now regrets. 'I refused to speak French because I said it wasn't science,' he says. 'And then I ended up working in Geneva [at CERN], where they speak French, so...' He joked that if he had continued with the foreign language then he would have been able to order meals at his workplace.

By all accounts, he kept himself to himself during the first couple of years at Oldham Hulme, concentrating on plane spotting. Because of his grandparents' and parents' sacrifice, he didn't like getting detentions and was careful not to disappoint. 'Certainly my impression of him over the first couple of years when our paths did cross was that he was just very quiet, quite studious, just very involved in cracking on with school work,' says Haughton. However, things began to change seriously around the age of 15. Cox had always been interested in music, especially the technological side, as we have since seen. His mother asked him to chaperone his sister Sandra to see Duran Duran play a concert in Leeds. 'It was the *Seven and the Ragged Tiger* tour,' he recalled. 'I thought, that looks brilliant, so I learned to play the keyboards.'

In fact, Duran Duran ended up being the first band he got into in a big way. Years later after he became famous, he met band member Nick Rhodes socially a number of times to talk about CERN and quantum theory, and they ended up as friends. It took him several meetings before he felt able to reveal the level of his fandom, though. Rhodes just laughed. 'Although I'd seen concerts before, this was the first Beatlemania-type thing – that atmosphere of screaming girls,' he explained. 'So I was just blown away by this spectacle and that's the moment I thought I want to be a pop star. So, the first thing to deflect me from the geeky pursuits of physics.'

The keyboards appealed to Cox's scientific nature. It was the early 1980s and electronic sounds were beginning to dominate the records in the charts. But he never took lessons (although the school did offer piano tuition) and instead taught himself. 'I was good at programming the keyboards,' he told Shortlist, 'but I never saw myself as a musician.' Around this time, he began listening to Billy Joel's 'New York State Of Mind'. 'When I started really wanting to play the piano, Billy Joel and Elton John were two big influences because I used to sit there and play along to these songs,' he told Kirsty Young on Radio 4's *Desert Island Discs*. 'If I sit down at a piano and I can't think of anything to do, then I play "New York State Of Mind."'

At the age of 11, he and a friend had listened to Ultravox and Kraftwerk mainly because of the electronic nature, but now Cox began to see the music, or rather pop stardom, as being a pathway to fame, fortune and girls. Enamoured of the techniques that went into creating the music, he immediately formed a band with a friend who lived up the road. Electronic music in those days was a geeky hobby and he tried to replicate the sounds generated by the band Orchestral Manoeuvres in the Dark (OMD) on their first album, *Messages*. OMD was the first concert he ever attended. He found a sympathetic partner in physics master Peter Galloway, who he later described to *The Times* as being his favourite teacher. 'Though he looked like a Seventies' physicist, complete with beard, Mr Galloway was very young, relaxed and different from most of the other teachers,' Cox remembered. 'What was great is you could sit down with him after school and say "I want to build this piece of electronics" and he would help you. One of the bands we liked was Ultravox and they had found a way to trigger chords on a keyboard to make it syncopate with a hi-hat drum. We wanted to make the same noise and needed to build something called a "noise gate" that would be triggered by the hi-hat. We asked Mr Galloway about it and he sat down and drew a circuit. Then we built the circuit with him and it worked. Years later I met Billy Currie, the keyboard player with Ultravox, and told him: "We had to build this thing with our physics teacher." And he said: "I know, I did the same." It was the only solution at the time for making that sound.'

It was also ironic considering one of his future bandmates in the group Dare, Vinny Burns, also went on to play with Ultravox. Peter Galloway was in his first year of teaching when he came across Cox. 'Brian was in his first year in the sixth form when I started teaching him,' he says. 'I remember him well – he always looked very boyish and he still looks just the same. To a certain extent he was just like all the other boys – sometimes he didn't do his homework or would be talking in class – but he wasn't at all bad. He was very inquisitive and bright, and seemed very keen on the topic.'

With music on his mind, it's no surprise that Cox started hanging out with a new crowd. He became a huge fan of David Bowie, especially the musician's 1971 album, *Hunky Dory*. In 2011, he chose 'Queen Bitch' as one of his songs on Radio 4's *Desert Island Discs*, saying: 'It always has been my favourite album for as long as I can remember. The musicianship is brilliant. Rick Wakeman, who's one of my favourite piano players, plays on the album. I could have chosen any track on *Hunky Dory*.' He also began buying 7" singles. One of the first was The Jam's "Going Underground". 'I must have been asking my mum and dad for the money,' he recalled. 'I absolutely loved it, played it over and over again. And I think it not only stands up, it's still brilliant.'

Tim Haughton remembers Oldham Hulme Grammar as being pretty disciplined and as you might imagine, it became a case of seeing how hard the students could push against those boundaries. 'The boys and the girls weren't supposed to mix,' he says, 'although we often tried to do so. People would meet halfway down a driveway and chat before you got caught and sent on your way.' Cox began mixing with a gang of boys who lived in the Saddleworth/Uppermill area and it was there that he came into contact with Haughton in a more social setting. 'You didn't just change groups because your friends changed, it tended to be what you were into,' adds Haughton. 'And we were all into the New Romantic thing. We went down the route of winklepicker shoes, long hair, big flickers [quiffed hair] – pants were a bit baggy in the top, bit tight in the bottom, that kind of thing. Brian had gone down that whole route: he had the big flicker, winklepicker shoes. He came out of his shell a little bit, started mingling more with the girls' school. Girls became a much more important facet of our everyday life, as did finding an off licence that would sell you a sneaky bottle of beer!'

Cox and his friends followed the music of Duran Duran, Roxy Music and The Human League. Haughton remembers them trying to emulate the hair of Phil Oakey, lead singer of the latter band. 'I used to have a huge flicker, but [Brian's] was there or thereabouts,' he laughs. 'We were competing.' At the same time, they started to embellish their school uniform: the tie got shorter and shorter, the trousers more fashionable. Though they were supposed to buy their clothes from specific local shops, they ignored the rules and concentrated on what was trendy. 'I seem to remember Brian having a cracking pair of winklepicker shoes, which had a longer point on them than anybody else's,' says Haughton.

Even though Cox was beginning to rebel a bit more, school work remained important, as did not getting in trouble. 'I regarded him as one of the really clever ones,' says classmate Joanne Smithies. 'I don't remember him to ever be in trouble – just a good kid, really.' He hung out in a group of around ten kids, who stuck pretty close together, but continued to enjoy his studies, especially those taught by people who had a unique perspective on teaching and indeed life. Few were quite as unique as Stephen 'Sam' Bell, a school legend who taught chemistry, though. Most were terrified of him and ditched the class when they heard they were to be taught by him. Someone who made lots of money as an amateur stock trader and paid for many extra-curricular activities in the school out of his own pocket (including the film club where Cox, aged 11, had seen *Alien*) as well as donating a Steinway piano and a harpsichord, Mr Bell stuck in Cox's mind during an interview with *The Times*. 'He was a perfectionist,' he recalled. 'You had to do everything very precisely. He used to go mental if anyone did anything wrong and practical experiments could clash with his control-freakery. If anyone sprayed copper sulphate out of a test tube, he would scream and throw people out of a lesson. When you were 11, you would all be frightened to death of him but by the time you were 15, everyone was fond of him because he was so strange. He would horrify educationalists today but he got amazing results. His approach was quite modern because he taught you to pass the exam with precision.'

While Cox was still conscientious in the classroom, away from it he was beginning to explore what it meant to be a teenager. Part of this coincided with both his grandparents dying when he was 14; he dabbled with dying his hair purple and becoming a Goth. 'I wonder now whether I'd have considered being in a band or gone through the Goth stage if they'd not died,' he told the *Daily Mail*. 'My sister tells me I was quite a handful.' Says Tim Haughton: 'On the outskirts of the school we had what you call the Maths wing, which was a prefab building of four classrooms. Teachers didn't tend to venture there that much during lunch hours and breaks, so that's where everyone tended to go to smoke and try and hook up with girls. Nearby to that was a driveway that ran the full length of the school and either end was where you could have contact with the girls from the girls' school. That was the place you tended to congregate when you got older.'

Despite living so close to a thriving metropolis like Manchester, Cox's social life didn't tend to stretch that far. 'Oldham was grim,' recalls Haughton. 'You didn't have places to go; you didn't have bowling alleys. You had cinemas but they were horrible, old crappy places. If I went into Manchester, it was at the weekend and I told them I was going into Oldham, and Oldham was a bit of a push. We didn't have the facility to have big adventures as such; you were very limited as to what you could do. You were relying on people's parents going out to have a sneaky party. When you look back, it would be awful to say we were nondescript but we were all just trying make fun in a fairly grim town; that one of the gang has gone on to bigger and better things is phenomenal.' Parties were generally local. 'It was a group of lads who lived around Saddleworth, Greenfield, that neck of the woods,' Haughton explains. 'More often than not, you went to somebody's house. If I look back now, we seemed to spend an inordinate amount of time sitting in what was called Mumps Bus Station. When I look back now, I couldn't tell you *why* we spent so much time there. It was under cover, but it was grim and there was no way we spent that much time there waiting for a bus.'

With his baby face, Cox didn't have much luck when it came to buying alcohol and required a bit more subterfuge. 'There was an off licence on Huddersfield Road, it was a bit of a walk for us,' Haughton continues. 'But you could go in with a little note that one of you'd written saying "Please will you let my son buy 20 Benson & Hedges". Or "please accept this letter as permission to sell my son a bottle of wine, which I require for my own purposes". Absolute nonsense! That's what we used to do. We'd spend amounts of time wandering along to shops we knew would sell us cigarettes or booze. We'd probably hang around outside arguing who was going in, who looked the oldest, who would get served – and basically panicking about it.'

There were also women. 'You've got to imagine at 14, 15 years old, the girls are starting to be interesting and you've been separated from them by this door that you know leads into their school, but you're never allowed to go through it,' adds Haughton. 'Suddenly, you're getting invited to a party and you're mixing together. It's like somebody's dropped a hormone bomb – that's what it was like. I don't remember anyone having steady girlfriends. Maybe when you're 17, 18, you had steadier girlfriends. But [before] it was a case of you went to a party and met somebody, snogged them, felt them up a little bit. They were your girlfriend for a couple of weeks and then it was somebody else – it was a very fluid situation.'

Though Haughton cannot remember specifics about Cox's longer-term female friends ('There probably are a couple of stories which I wouldn't tell you because it wouldn't be appropriate for me to do so! A gentleman never tells.'), one incident does stick out in his mind. 'I remember him snogging this girl on the back of the bus one night coming out of Oldham, heading back towards Greenfield. What's the polite way to put this? She wasn't particularly attractive, but she was known to be, er, quite easy. I seem to remember she had vaguely ginger hair, I suppose you'd call it strawberry blonde now. I've got a real feeling her name was Katherine. I should clarify when we were 15/16, easy wasn't getting your pants off. Easy was letting you have a feel over the bra and over the top – that was considered a result. I'm not suggesting she was legs akimbo on the back seat of the bus,' he laughs. 'Those girls tended to be particularly popular.'

What Cox didn't seem to talk about once he reached a certain age was work. Rather, it was something that he carried on doing quietly, away from his friends. Nor did he initially share his desire to pursue music on a more long-term basis with them, at least not in any serious way. In fact, Haughton doesn't recall him being particularly musical at all, or at least not ostentatious about it. 'You blend into the group you're in,' he says of being a teenager. 'Anything that separates you, you try and avoid that as much as you possibly can – it's all about trying to fit in. If all your mates are talking about these girls, it might be the thing that interests you, but all you talk about is girls because that's the conversation.' And fit in he did. 'I would say 90 per cent of our conversation was women. Probably another 4 or 5 per cent was "isn't school terrible?" and which off licence would sell us a bottle of Yates's Original Wine, which tasted absolutely awful, but got you absolutely plastered. There was very little conversation about anything which involved academia.'

Away from the school gang, though, Cox was thinking about his future. Even then, he was considering media as a career choice if music didn't work out. In one particular case, he tried to combine the two. Cox has talked about doing work experience on Piccadilly Radio in Manchester as a teenager; how he was 15 and there to answer phones, while sharing an office with broadcaster Chris Evans, then another lowly intern. But the DJ he worked for – children's TV favourite, Timmy Mallett – remembers it slightly differently. Mallett recalls a young man walking into his *Timmy On The Tranny* show with loftier ambitions. 'At age 17, he'd shown up in a rock star T-shirt, a mop of wild hair and a big smile, clutching keyboards,' he described in one of his Brilliant TV podcasts. 'He was the glamorous boyfriend of one of our phone call takers. "Brian's got some jingles for you" she said, and as usual, I grilled him, had a listen, told him to work on them and come back when they were great. He grinned, agreed and did.' According to Mallett, they became Cox's first musical success. 'We used them on Piccadilly's award-winning night-time pop show,' said the presenter. 'Now Brian's a star scientist, expounding the wonders of the universe on television, living his dream. If we ever find those jingles – and they will be somewhere – on an old cassette tape in someone's loft, we'll have a laugh and recall the enthusiasm and adventure that went into having a chance and seizing it.' Chances are, Cox hopes they will never be found.

Despite all this, he still intended to go to university and sat four A-levels: maths, chemistry, physics and general studies. He did well in the latter three, but found mathematics especially hard. 'I found out quite late in life that I could do maths,' he said later. 'I didn't like maths at all in school, but I did it because I liked physics and I thought I had to do it.' It wasn't until later that he realised if he treated maths like a craft, a musical instrument, something he had to practice and spend hours doing, that he could do it. He dedicated himself to understanding equations and doing the workings and gradually became better and better. However, at A-level, he got a D grade. It must have been especially difficult receiving his grade, since maths does seem to be so central to anyone who wants to pursue physics or science as a career. By that point, however, music had already begun to take over his life and the idea of becoming a pop star was firmly in his head. 'I was at a gig in Manchester the night before [my maths A-level] and went straight from there,' he said. 'But I got an A in physics, so I just being lazy, really. I was thinking, it doesn't matter what I get in my A-levels because I'm going to be a musician.'

He would worry about quadratic equations later. School friend Tim Haughton certainly doesn't remember Cox obsessing over his grades or schoolwork. 'A lot of people look at someone like Brian and think geek,' he says, 'must have been, somebody who has got that level of knowledge and is into these things. But he just wasn't. Although that was my initial impression of him, that he was geeky and studious, he certainly wasn't as I remember him 14, 15 years old onwards. He was quite the partygoer, just a really down-to-earth regular lad. I remember him being a really good laugh, very much one of the lads. Awesome winklepickers!'

It's worth pointing out not everyone at school had great respect for Cox. Definitely not the anonymous Facebooker, who created a page called 'I urinated in Brian Cox's school bag'. While it may be tempting to pass this off as a shameless social networking gag, there's a mention of a teacher's name – on the page Ben Counsel, but most likely meant to be Bernard Counsel, who was certainly a teacher at Oldham Hulme. A relative of Counsel's even phoned up while Cox was on Radio 2 in 2011 to point out the fact that Counsel was one of his masters. You can decide how realistic this 'anecdote' may be.

Yet the question with famous people and their school days is always the same: could you tell he was going to be a celebrity when he was just a teenager? Not so, according to Tim Haughton. 'Funnily enough, I met up with some guys from school a month or so ago and that was a topic of conversation,' he says. 'The honest answer is not really, no. Clearly Brian's an intelligent lad but then there were other people in the group who were always the joker, very confident. Not as intelligent as Brian, but the kind of guys who you could imagine popping up on TV one morning.' He remembers hearing Cox's name again, years later, when he was a part of dance outfit D:Ream. 'D:Ream, with the nicest will in the world, were a one-hit wonder,' says Haughton. 'They had so much success with that one song. And you thought, this has got to be the springboard to much greater things and they just disappeared off the face of the planet. You expect that people get one bite of the cherry with that sort of thing. And yet years later, here he is again.

Everyone was dead chuffed for him. He's a nice guy. Who doesn't begrudge somebody decent doing well for themselves? We had a bit of a giggle about it, really.'

Another person close to the school who wishes to remain anonymous echoes these sentiments. 'He was obviously a bright chap and a bit unconventional, [but] I wouldn't have known he was going to turn out like that,' he says. 'To be fair, he's got the right manner and he's just got the breaks.'

Having Brian Cox, the famous TV physicist, as a former pupil has only meant good things for the school itself. It continues to thrive (and the door between the girls and boys has since been removed!) and a number of the pupils study science beyond A-levels. 'He's been very good, not just for the school but for science,' says one source. Another admits the school benefits from being Cox's alma mater. 'I think it does,' he says. 'Certainly the fact Brian Cox is big news at the moment. I think it does help; it's nice for us. He mentions us and that he mentioned Peter [Galloway] as an inspiration is nice. [The school] are still in touch with him and he has promised he will come back at some point, which would be fantastic, but he can't commit himself that far in the future.'

So, Cox left school with a keyboard under his arm and dreams of stardom. Little did he know it was brewing just down the round from his parents' house.

CHAPTER 3

DARE TO WIN

It's not every day a rock star moves in round the corner from your house, especially if you lived near Oldham in the mid-1980s. So, word spread quickly when Darren Wharton, former keyboard player of legendary rock group Thin Lizzy, took ownership of a property close where Cox and his family lived. Not only that, but Wharton – a curly-haired, handsome man in his early- to mid-twenties – began drinking in the same pub as Brian's father and before long, the former Lizzy-ite knew about the teenage Cox and his musical aspirations. We need to back up a bit first, though because the story of Dare, Cox's real musical interlude from science and the band which almost deprived the BBC of its face of physics, starts a couple of years earlier.

Lancastrian Darren Wharton was a keyboard player and songwriter who as a teenager had been discovered playing in Manchester nightclubs and was recruited by legendary rock'n'roll band Thin Lizzy to play in one of their latter incarnations. But as Lizzy frontman Phil Lynott's addictions took hold and the group disintegrated around 1984, Wharton found himself back in his hometown of Chadderton near Oldham, in a nice 18th-century farmhouse purchased from the proceeds of various rock records. Keen to make the transition to frontman and singer, Wharton turned down offers from other groups and signed a deal with Phonogram records as a solo artist. Following this, he set about putting together a band. He found lead guitarist Vinny Burns through a friend and the pair worked on material for about six months before beginning to sign up other members. Working under Wharton's name, they hired Ed Stratton on drums and a BBC sound engineer with the single moniker Shelly on bass. They took photos and began rehearsing, but then Wharton's deal with Phonogram fell through and the band found themselves without record company backing. Stratton was sacked – he didn't get on with Shelly and also lived far away from the other guys in Northampton – and local lad Jim Ross drafted in on drums.

Wharton was also keen to change the band's name to something else. While at Donington, he bumped into Lemmy from Motorhead and confided in him. Lemmy suggested Dare 1. Wharton didn't like the numeral, so dropped it and Dare was born. Burns and Wharton continued to write and record songs, doing a deal with a studio in Manchester whereby they would play for free on radio idents and jingles; in return, Dare would get to record or rehearse in the studio. Until now, Wharton had been singing from behind a keyboard, but he now wanted more freedom of movement and decided to hire a second keyboard player, while using Eighties staple the keytar (Wharton's version, which he fashioned himself using lashings of gaffer tape was dubbed 'The Batmobile'). A youngster called Mark Simpson was hired and the band, which was starting to pick up momentum locally, continued to gig furiously. Record companies began to take an interest and Chrysalis were potentially keen to sign them; the band travelled to London for a showcase but the head of A&R at Chrysalis wasn't interested. They recorded several demos and found their manager, Keith Aspden after he was introduced to them by someone who worked in that studio. However, the band ended up going their separate ways.

It was 1986 and Brian Cox was getting ready to go to university. He would drive around in his souped-up Ford Fiesta, listening to the music from *Top Gun* until he hit a lamp post and got charged for it by Oldham Council. He began listening to something more sedate. Aware of the rock star living round the corner and with a decent grasp of the keyboards, he had dropped a tape round to Wharton's house a couple of years before. More importantly, Cox's dad went to the same pub as the singer and had been round to his house a few times. 'They talked about music,' says fan Mick Taylor, whose love for the group led him to become head of the Dare fan club. When Mark Simpson left the band, Wharton remembered the tape he'd received and asked Cox Sr whether his son still played keyboards. With his spiky hair and sharp cheekbones, Cox certainly looked like a rock star. 'I would say without a doubt Brian was the best-looking one,' recalls Taylor. 'You only need to look at pictures when he was in Dare and he was the heartthrob – he stood out like a sore thumb. My ex-missus said he was the best-looking!'

Wharton offered Cox – five-and-a-half-years his junior – a place in the band. Though he still had dreams of being a scientist, the 18-year-old didn't think it would be too bad to take a year off and give rock stardom a go. It turned out to be a lot longer. 'You don't miss physics when you're 18, in a rock and roll band,' he once reminisced. Surprisingly, his parents didn't mind the diversion. 'They were actually really supportive,' he told Radio 4. 'They loved watching us live. They came to Manchester Apollo to see us and really enjoyed the process – I think they were quite upset when the band split up and I went to university. I think they enjoyed their time in the rock and roll sun.' The Maple Squash Club in Oldham, near the football ground, became the band's home from home. They knew the owners, Allan and Rita, who let them rehearse free of charge and soon they had a Saturday night residency at the venue.

'We used to go every week,' remembers Oldham resident Tony Steel, an early Dare follower. 'We got hooked. It was before the first album, so they used to do all the stuff from the first album at the gigs.' Steel is just one of the many fans who fell in love with the group from the start. 'It was quite a small room, quite a low ceiling,' he says of the Squash Club, which held about 100 people. 'It was a bar/restaurant – very close, very personal. It was a great atmosphere, because it was rock, but you could hear the music and the words they were singing.' The audience tended to be around the same age as the band and despite the loud music and the alcohol on offer, there wasn't any fighting. 'It was the same people, week in week out,' says Steel.

'[The band] brought their friends. It was the same faces. Then it grew a little bit each week to the point where if you didn't get there by eight o'clock, you didn't get in.'

The gigs were where the band honed their stage act. 'Darren was confident because he had toured all over the world,' recalls Steel. 'Brian was a bit shy because he was the youngest one. He didn't tend to speak – he stood in the back, hiding behind his keyboards. I remember him being quite shy compared to Darren Wharton and Vinny Burns. You could tell [Brian] was doing most of the keyboards. They all did little solo bits and you could tell he was actually playing it. He wasn't just in the background for shows. He had long hair at the back and spiky on top. Not like punk spiky – the whole top was spiked up, a proper mullet – the usual Eighties band thing.'

Cox himself remembers 'long hair, hairspray, ripped jeans, leather jackets…' He would become transfixed watching Wharton cover himself in what he thought was chip fat before shows. 'He used to grease himself up and run around!' he laughed. 'We were very Eighties.' Unlike many of the acts in those days, the keyboard set-up was pretty small. Some of this was to do with the fact they already had two keyboard players but also because they couldn't really afford any equipment. Shelly had to borrow a bass before every gig. It wasn't until their record deal that they could splash out on new gear and any fees collected from the early shows were used to pay for a van to travel to the venues. Sometimes they even had to resort to dubious means to get around the transportation issue. 'When I first started publishing a fanzine for Dare, I advertised it in the music papers,' explains Mick Taylor. 'Not long afterwards, I got a letter that had been sent from Her Majesty's Prison Strangeways in Manchester. It was from a loveable rogue called Ian McGiffen, who introduced himself as Dare's road manager. He had got himself into some trouble, so was temporarily unavailable!

'Ian has sadly passed away now, but he told me that one day he was on tour with Dare and they were due to travel to a gig one night but their van had broken down; they were stuck. Ian was one step ahead and told the guys not to worry. A couple of hours later, he turned up with this van saying he had borrowed it from a mate but had to have it back the same day. The guys loaded up the van and off they went. After the gig had finished, Ian dropped everyone off and took the van back to where he had *stolen* it, ha ha! Little did the band know they were travelling around in a stolen van! Ian was very proud of his time with Dare and Darren later wrote a song with him in mind called 'Breakout', which was on the band's second album, *Blood From Stone.'*

The Maple residency lasted almost 18 months and meanwhile the band continued to increase their following around the northwest. Cox dubbed them the 'Oldham Bon Jovi'. They had a small crew, including Burns' brother Russ and Ian McGiffen, and the shows were beginning to feel slicker, with good sound and a quality light show. In fact, they even managed to swing a 12-day tour of Hong Kong after a photographer friend lied to a promoter about who they were. It was only the second time Cox had been abroad (the first was a school ski trip). They did some gigs and appeared on a local TV show before heading back, where they were greeted with increased record company interest. It was the first time Cox appeared on television, smiling shyly from behind his keyboards. Amazingly, it looked like his dreams of becoming a rock star might just come true – and sooner than he thought.

'I wouldn't say it was dead easy,' says Mick Taylor, but by all accounts three companies were fighting to land the band's signature. EMI came to see them at a gig in Oldham and then MCA checked out a concert at the Maple Squash Club. RCA and A&M got wind that both labels were interested, so immediately headed up to watch the group perform the following week. Convinced they had found the next big thing, A&M told the boys to forget the rest and drew up an eight-album deal. In May 1987, Cox was a member of a band with a record deal and any ideas of becoming a scientist would have to be put on hold.

Though Dare had acquired a reputation as a formidable local live act, all they had to show for it as far as recordings went were some demos. 'It was before mobile phones, so you couldn't record it and play it back as you could do now,' explains Tony Steel. There were live bootlegs kicking around, but not many. A&M were keen to get an album in the bag and into the shops, so they introduced the lads to Mike Shipley and Larry Klein, the duo who would produce their first album. Shipley was an Australian who had moved to Los Angeles in 1984 and worked with hundreds of acts as a sound engineer, including AC/DC and The Clash. Klein was a former session bass player, who had married folk singer Joni Mitchell and moved into producing. Dare had plenty of tracks ready to go – in fact, they already had the core of their first record. In January 1988, they all piled, hungover, into Cox's Ford Fiesta and headed off to Hookend

Manor in Berkshire, a mansion formerly owned by Pink Floyd's Dave Gilmour that had since become a favourite recording haunt of music labels. They laid down some tracks, but the producers decided they needed to finish off the album in LA, so the band headed out there. It didn't take much persuasion.

They stayed at the Sheraton Miramar in Santa Monica and recorded at Joni Mitchell's property in Bel Air. 'It was really fantastic,' recalled Cox. But it wasn't all rock'n'roll. During a day off, the band decided to visit Disneyland, south of the city. They drove their hire car down there and parked it in one of the huge parking lots. After enjoying the rides, they returned to pick up their car, only they couldn't recall where they had parked it. Remembering the area for parked cars was the 'size of Leeds', Cox has said: 'all we knew was that it was red!' He added: 'We had to wait until everyone had gone home and there was nothing left in the parking lot. And then they drove us around until we saw a red car. We had to wait until about midnight. That's rock and roll, isn't it? Lost in Disneyland!'

In those days, it was also crucial to make a video to accompany a single and with 'Abandon' chosen as the first song to be released off the debut album, the band returned to Los Angeles in August of the same year to shoot the promo. It was filmed in South Central LA, a down-at-heel part of downtown (especially so in 1988) and features the group rocking out against an industrial backdrop and lots of dry ice. Somewhat inexplicably, a sexy young woman (actually future *Twin Peaks* star Mädchen Amick, who would go on to become a successful TV actress in particular) meanders about, showing off her cleavage before climbing into a fancy car, supposedly having been abandoned. The video ends with the guys walking off into a smoke-filled distance. Cox doesn't get all that much screen time as it is mainly focused on Wharton and Burns but there's a moment when he can definitely be seen grinning. Considering what he might have been doing at the time had he not been shooting a rock video, it's unsurprising.

A&M unveiled the band before the press on 25 October 1988 at The Marquee Club in Soho. As this was the group's debut London show, they were understandably nervous. It wasn't helped by a poor sound mix, which often drowned out the vocals. The record company were careful to mix the media in with a group of supporters from Manchester, so that it wasn't simply an anodyne showcase. Journalist Valerie Potter – a self-confessed Dare fan – was there and wrote: 'The band were obviously rigid with nerves and this made their performance a little shaky until they got into their stride. Nevertheless, I still stoutly maintain that this band is one to watch for in '89. Second keyboard player Brian Cox puts in some sterling support from the back of the stage. There are still some rough edges that need to be smoothed away by regular gigging, but now that Dare have leapt over the hurdle of the "debut London show", on their next London appearance, I think they'll show us what they can *really* do.'

The band thought they had done a decent job. Vinny Burns later wrote: 'We played it very safe and it felt more like being in a goldfish bowl than any of the other good Marquee gigs that we would play later on. The press seemed to go on more about the fact that A&M had done an over-the-top free bar for guests – we couldn't even get served with free drinks ourselves, it was that packed. We knew we would be footing the bill for it all in the long run; we made sure that didn't happen again. Still, it was good to play the Marquee and it was a good gig, too.'

'Abandon' was the first single to be released but it didn't do very well, only reaching No. 99 in the charts when it originally came out (it spent two weeks getting to No. 71 when re-released in July, the following year). It had a couple of champions, though and for the fans, this felt like the start of great things. 'It was a real shock to the system first time we heard it on the radio,' remembers fan Tony Steel. 'We started hearing it on Radio 1. There was a teatime DJ, Gary Davies. I remember him saying he was going to play something from a new band and it was one of the best intros he'd ever heard. That was "Abandon" and it *is* a fantastic intro.' The fact that they were a local band made good made it all the more special for those who had been there right from the beginning. 'It was like, "I know these, I used to go and watch these,"' adds Steel. 'It was quite a proud moment in that we'd helped them get there. If we hadn't gone to watch them, they would have never made it – we felt part of the success.'

And the fans weren't the only ones who were shocked. 'Obviously there was a big fuss about him joining the group and having a single coming out,' says school friend, Tim Haughton. 'At the time, everyone thought it was a load of bullshit, to be honest with you. Everyone thought he was just talking it up and it would never happen, blowing his own trumpet. And then obviously it happened and everyone was like, "oh my God, he's telling the truth!" One thing you've got in a school like that is you've a lot of intelligent people, there's a lot of egos involved –

you couldn't go a week without someone starting a band, but a week later it had all dissolved into nothing. So, when someone says "I'm in this band, we're going to be bringing a single out, we're going into the studio and recording some songs", everyone goes "yeah, great, what a lot of bullshit!" When it actually happened, everyone was gobsmacked.'

The album, titled *Out of the Silence*, was released not long afterwards. Because of a quirk in the Gallup charting system, which said only certain stores were counted as being valid for sales, it didn't make the charts. Fans have pointed out that 89 per cent of the LP's sales came from the Greater Manchester area and sometimes it was selling up to 300 copies per day. If that was the case, it would have been a Top Five record. It received positive reviews from the music press, with Jon Hotten in heavy metal bible *Kerrang!* giving it four and three-quarter stars out of five. 'Dare have everything,' he wrote. 'Songs, instrumentation, production, but most of all they have that indefinable X ingredient that sets them apart and above the rest. Take "Abandon", build around rich keyboards and vocal hooks that will tear you apart, but the album's high point is without a doubt "Under the Sun", a supreme example of dramatic atmosphere and how to create it around a lilting, minor-key piano accompaniment. Dare are there to be awed and AOR fans will lap it up. As a genre piece this excels and I love it. Don't miss it.'

Elsewhere, the keyboards parts were described as 'shimmering' while another critic added: 'the keyboards and guitars blended together nicely'. The album went Top 20 in Sweden and Cox's youthful looks were noticed by some writers: 'The man with the perpetual grin and baby face, which makes me wonder if he'll ever start shaving,' scribbled one hack. During live shows, Wharton continued to play his keytar, mainly because of the rich keyboard sounds on the album. 'It was either that or use tapes,' he told one magazine. 'Brian couldn't physically play what was on the album alone.' Some articles go so far to suggest that Cox mostly played the rhythm lines on the record, while Wharton did the majority of the lead solo work. Certainly he did some solos while onstage, but it's clear Cox did pull his weight. 'It was more Darren and Vinny who wrote the songs,' says fan club chief and aficionado Mick Taylor. 'But I did go to watch them in the studios once, I think it was called The Greenhouse Studios, when they were rehearsing. You'd get Brian adding a little keyboard part and saying "what do you think of this?" So in a way, he was involved, putting his ideas in. But it was actually Darren and Vinny who wrote all the songs.'

For Cox, life was good. And the band was tight: despite their growing success, they remained good Northern boys at heart. One fan called Rob Till remembers missing his train after a gig, when the guys allowed him to sleep on the floor of their hotel. There were girls, too. Says Mick Taylor: 'Obviously, there were groupies and that sort of thing.' They indulged as you might expect, but Cox later insisted it was not so hardcore as some of their heavy metal contemporaries. 'There were a few [groupies],' he said, 'although I was probably too naïve to notice at the time – I probably would have made more use if I had been older.' He told Shortlist: 'We were just a bunch of lads from Oldham who got a deal. If you're 20 years old and you get plonked in the middle of LA with an expenses account, you're going to have a drink, aren't you? It was all quite innocent, really. I never crashed my Rolls-Royce into a swimming pool or anything – I had a rusty Ford Fiesta. And no pool to drive it into.'

With the advance they received, they paid themselves £75 a week and gradually increased this to £120. 'We thought – "my God, we've made it!"' They favoured Henry's Wine Bar in Manchester and even impressed George Harrison. 'After a gig one night we were sat in a bar and [Darren] saw this guy pushing in, so he told him to f*** off,' Cox told *Metro*. 'It was George Harrison. George said, "I haven't been told to f*** off since 1965" and was so impressed, he bought us all a drink.'

Taylor, later the boss of their fan club, met the band around this time. 'I was working at MFI in Rochdale,' he remembers. 'Me and my friend used to swap tapes with each other. One day he left a tape on my desk by Dare, who I'd never heard of. I listened to the tape and it was brilliant, so I asked him who they were. He said his wife's cousin was called Darren Wharton and used to be in Thin Lizzy. I got that much into them that I started making a scrapbook. I went to see them live at a gig in Oldham. Unfortunately, they wouldn't let me backstage, but I was with my friend and he was, so I left my scrapbook with him and asked if he could get the band to sign it. The next day at work, my friend said they were impressed with my scrapbook and next time I went to a gig, I should go and introduce myself. So that's what I did. I went on tour with them and managed to get backstage passes all the time. In the end, Darren Wharton asked me if I'd run the fan club.'

Though Taylor tended to mix primarily with Wharton and

Burns, he grew to know the rest of the band as well. 'When I first met all of them, they were all quite young,' he says. 'Brian was the youngest in the band and the shy one, really. I wouldn't expect in a million years that years later he'd be "Professor Brian Cox". Back then no one knew that Brian was into science or what he was doing – he was just seen as a pop idol, if you know what I mean. He wasn't the most talkative one. Obviously I did talk to Brian, but he was the quiet one in the band. I wouldn't say it was hard to get him into a conversation, but he'd only answer questions that you asked him. It wasn't that he was miserable – I think it was because I got myself more involved with Darren and Vinny and the other three members were in the background. It was a "hiya", a shake of the hand and a nod of the head.'

A&M were keen to get the band playing more venues around the UK and abroad – especially on the continent, where rock music was particularly popular. In November 1988, they were sent out as a support act for Jimmy Page, ex-guitarist of Led Zeppelin for his UK dates. Neonbubble.com posted a humorous interview with Cox, in which he described his favourite hotel, talking about a place he stayed in while on tour with Page in Newcastle. 'I can't remember the name of the hotel but let me tell you this: mirrors on both sides of the bathroom!' he said. 'Luxury! You could look in one and see a reflection, and a reflection of a reflection and so on. In fact, I tried an experiment there by waving and seeing how long it would be before the distant reflections waved back – it was a test of the speed of light and how drunk I was – but some of the reflections didn't wave at all and I got scared. That's when I knew I'd never watch *Poltergeist 3* again. And the towels were really fluffy – stole two.'

For the group, playing with Page was something of a dream come true, especially at the Manchester Apollo, the scene of many gigs they had watched as teenagers. They even got to see how realistic *Spinal Tap* was at a concert in Birmingham. 'We did our set [at the Hummingbird],' wrote Vinny Burns. 'Jimmy came to our dressing room to say he enjoyed our show. He went out of the door and was about to walk down the steps to the stage (his intro was running). Darren shouted, "Have a good one, Jimmy!" and as he turned round to say thanks, he fell down the stairs. Oops! We were waiting to be booted off the tour but everything was fine.'

It's hard to quantify just how successful Dare were in those early days but they had a solid live following. 'If you went to a gig, the queues would be right round the block,' says Mick Taylor. 'I can't understand why they weren't huge. When we went to a Dare gig, it was brilliant. They'd get the crowd going and everyone was bouncing around – it was like a personal gig, in a way. It wasn't like the stage was forty feet away and they were up twenty feet: they were there and you could actually touch the band.' As well as their live reputation, *Out of the Silence* sold an impressive 50,000 copies in America ('quite big, considering they were an unknown band,' explains Taylor). And the critics liked them. Yet for some reason they didn't quite break through.

'I asked Darren why they didn't go to the States to advertise their CD, but he said it was down to management,' says Taylor. 'They had poor management, really – that's why they didn't go to the States, or it might have been a different story today.' The singles, too never really took off in the UK. 'In England, the singles they released off the [first] CD did get in the low regions of the charts. It's a shame, really but they were a good band and they had a great following.' A second single, 'The Raindance', was released and got to No. 62 in the charts in April 1989. Distributed as a 7" gatefold vinyl, it featured five profile cards with trivia about the band members. Cox listed his pastimes as 'squash, running and eating'. And despite being rock stars, he did retain some of his middle-class roots, playing squash with Wharton most mornings, since they only lived half a mile apart in Chadderton.

The band continued to work hard. 'They did gig constantly,' recalls Taylor. 'I was surprised because when I first got into them, I'd go to one gig and think that's it for another few months and then I'd be walking around Manchester and there would be an advert for another.' While Brian and the guys were having fun, it never got too crazy. 'We weren't very rock and roll,' Cox told the *Sun*. 'The closest I got to mayhem was throwing a tea tray out of a window in a hotel room in Carlisle. We were only on the first floor and the teapot just bounced off the pavement next to a bemused passer-by. And we made sure to carefully open and close the window.'

The hotel was The Crown & Mitre in the city centre. So un-rock'n'roll was this particular episode that no one can remember it happening. 'Roy, who worked here at the time, know who the band is,' said a hotel spokesperson, 'but doesn't remember anyone doing that.' A&M booked them a slot as the openers for Swedish rockers Europe, then riding high in the charts with the follow-up to their mega-selling album, *The Final Countdown*. The 58-date *Out of this World* tour saw Dare tour across the continent, playing to packed stadiums of more than 12,000 people in places like Paris and Stockholm. 'This was one of the best times I have had on the road,' wrote Vinny Burns. 'The guys from Europe and all their crew were amazing. In over four months, there were no arguments between bands and the general vibe was a four-month party.'

The tour helped to improve Dare as a live outfit as they got used to the bigger venues. Wharton stopped using the Batmobile and being able to run around the stage meant their stage presence became even better. Shelly hooked up with Europe's wardrobe lady, while Cox got his second taste of televisual fame when one of the concerts was broadcast on RTL in Germany. At the last gig, Dare ran up onstage to cover the headliners in cream as a practical joke. And while no one following the band knew particularly of Cox's scientific inclination, it was clear that despite his musically enforced hiatus, it was never a subject far from his mind. 'I remember Brian Cox with his big smile and an inquisitive mind trying to figure out the science behind the famous "Final Countdown" keyboard sound,' says Europe frontman and founder Joey Tempest. 'A very humble and warm individual.'

The tour reached Britain in late March 1989, with dates at the Birmingham NEC and London Hammersmith Odeon. A&M released another single, "Nothing Is Stronger Than Love", which didn't chart. But the band were getting itchy feet about recording new material: while on tour, they had been writing new songs and were keen to put them on tape. There was also something of a split within the group. Bass player Shelly and drummer Jim Ross appeared to have fallen out of favour with the rest of the band and ended up being replaced. In an interview with *Hot Metal*, Cox revealed: 'By the time the final split came, Darren, Vinny and I had recorded about seven new songs, playing all the instruments between us.' Nigel Clutterbuck was brought in on bass, while Greg Morgan took over the drummer's slot.

Searching for a more layered sound, especially onstage, a young graduate from the Salford College of Music called Richard Dews was also hired as an extra guitarist. Cox survived the cull. 'He was very popular with Darren,' says Mick Taylor. 'In Darren's eyes it was Darren, Vinny and Brian – they were good friends.' Certainly, Cox was now considered one of the senior members of the band despite still being only just into his twenties. And he was keen to affirm that the new line-up only made Dare stronger. 'The whole band is so tight now, too,' he said. 'When we rehearse, we hardly need to do much of the old stuff because it's all there. We tend to concentrate more on developing new material, which we are hoping to do in the new set.' The band had been hinting at a different, heavier sound during their gigs, showcasing the new song 'Breakout'. They were also playing some Thin Lizzy covers. 'The crowd seemed to like it,' he said. 'I think it's just good fun. We're certainly now trading off the memory of Lizzy and considering Darren was in the band, we've got every right to perform a couple of their numbers.'

'Darren thought the crowd wanted them to go heavier,' says Taylor. '*Out of the Silence* was more melodic rock, but *Blood*

From Stone was heavy.' *Blood From Stone* was the group's sophomore effort and on top of a harder sound, also had elements of a Celtic influence, which would feed into the group's later records. It was recorded in Los Angeles with famed producer Keith Olsen, the man behind smash hits such as Whitesnake's 'Here I Go Again' and Rick Springfield's 'Jessie's Girl' and released in September 1991. A&M said: 'On a far heavier and unequivocally more representative album, [Dare] dispel for good the ill-fitting AOR title from their collective shoulders. The British have a fine musical tradition and when that tradition is enhanced by a passionate emerald hue, then you know that not only are you in for a consummate musical treat, but also that one of the very finest exponents is Dare.'

The critics were generally positive. It received four stars in *Kerrang!*, which wrote: 'Darren Wharton and guitarist Vinny Burns have retained only keyboards man Brian Cox (who doesn't have an awful lot to do anymore!).' The first single was 'We Don't Need A Reason', which was released a month earlier in August 1991 and reached No. 52. It was their highest-charting single. During an interview, one journalist compared *Blood From Stone* to the work of metal group Skid Row, much to the consternation of the band. 'It doesn't sound like Skid Row,' opined Wharton, with Cox adding: 'it doesn't say "fook" on it 18 times either!'

Meanwhile, they were still incredibly popular around their hometown. Fans flocked to the Golden Disc in Hilton Arcade to have albums, posters, jackets and more signed by the band and to catch a glimpse of the new line-up when the single 'Real Love' was released in October 1991. It spent one week in the chart at No. 67. Cox talked of a return to the Queen Elizabeth Hall in Oldham for a homecoming concert, which would far outstrip their previous performances there. They even tried to emulate the likes of Def Leppard, who had created alter egos for themselves, forcing one game journalist to call Cox 'Corky' throughout an interview.

Despite their protestations, it became clear that the end was nigh, though. 'A&M had done as much as they could and nothing was happening,' explains Mick Taylor. 'Then the manager left.' In retrospect, Wharton realised *Blood From Stone*'s new sound hadn't really worked. 'I hate to say it but we were all sheep back then,' he said subsequently. 'Looking back, it was definitely the wrong thing to do. We should have had the maturity not to jump on the bandwagon. As far as Dare are concerned, *Blood From Stone* was too much of a change in direction and we suffered for it in the end, really.'

The constant touring was beginning to take its toll, too. One time, a roadie called Drac led a team which ended up with Cox gaffer-taped to a lighting rig for over an hour. 'I was probably not behaving in a way deemed appropriate for a member of a band in the presence of road crew,' said Cox. 'I think I was just being a general, you know, pain. [Drac] was the tour manager, so he ordered the rest of the crew to put me on the ground, gaffer me up into a ball, put a harness on and then attach me to a lighting rig at the Hammersmith Odeon.' Asked whether he could remember what drove them to it, Cox replied: 'It was a build-up of absolute annoyance over many weeks.' The final tipping point came in Berlin. 'It was a proper fight,' said Cox. 'We were drunk and tired, and everyone just jumped on one another.' He elaborated to Shortlist: 'We'd been touring for four years and we were sick of each other. We all threw a few punches in a half-hearted way. Nobody's nose got broken; it was slapping, mainly – like those fights that footballers have. But it was enough to split up the band.'

A&M were on the verge of dropping Dare anyway because *Blood From Stone* was a massive change and it didn't do well at all.' Indeed, the album spent one week in the charts and got to No. 48. Wharton has suggested that A&M were bought by Polygram and that's why they were left out in the cold (in a strange echoing of his solo deal with Phonogram), but it didn't really matter: the record company dropped them and it was decision-making time. News of Burns' exit hit the music papers but was relayed to the heartbroken fans, along with a sad editorial about the split from A&M, in Dare's official fanzine #8. The edition also added: 'Brien (sic) is also leaving Dare! The reason for Brien (sic) leaving is that he is going to university some time this year, so we all wish Brian the best of luck, cheers mate.'

At first, despite Vinny leaving, it appeared that Cox would stick with Dare because Wharton suggested in an interview that he would continue working with the other members of the band. However, it's clear that once A&M got wind of the lead guitarist's departure and decided to terminate their contract, Cox decided it was time to get back to his academic pathway: 'I just decided that I would carry on doing physics,' he explained.

Dare did continue on. Not long after Cox left, they played Manchester Rockworld and he came to see them play. 'They're still going now,' says Taylor. 'Dare is really Darren Wharton and there have been various line-up changes, but Brian was there for the first two CDs.' Vinny Burns went on to join Asia and Ultravox and then became big in Japan as a member of Ten. The Maple Squash Club was torn down years ago and flats built in its place. NL Distribution re-released *Out of the Silence* in 2008, probably to capitalise on Cox's newfound fame. 'I've got four albums on my phone and I regularly listen to them,' says fan Tony Steel.

Taylor lost contact with Cox after he quit Dare. However, a random trip out with Darren Wharton after the band had split led to a mini reunion. 'I did actually see Brian in the pub once,' says Taylor. 'Brian was asking Darren how he did his different tones of voice – you know, when you harmonise in a studio? He wanted to know about octaves and things like that and how to do them. So he was obviously doing a bit of singing with D:Ream or something in the studio with them. That's the only time I've seen Brian after he left Dare.'

Cox's hair metal days were over. Despite being his entrance into the music business and a fundamental era in moving from young adult to grown-up, Dare are only ever mentioned as an afterthought in interviews with the scientist. Instead, he's known as the rock star physicist who played keyboards with D:Ream – ironic considering his position in Dare was far more substantive than in the late-Nineties dance act, as we'll explore. In fact, when asked about his time in pop, Cox himself set the record straight. 'My memory of music is not D:Ream,' he said. 'It's more this band Dare I was in.' The Maple Squash Club regulars will be glad to hear him say that. Despite leaving the band the long hair remained (and would so for a number of years), but it was time to head back to academia.

CHAPTER 4

UNIVERSITY IS
A D:REAM

It's funny that in almost every profile ever written about him, Brian Cox has become known as an ex-D:Ream band member. That's not to say it's not true; it is. But compared to the five years he slogged away in Dare, his brief sojourn into the actual fold of D:Ream between 1993 and 1994 was merely a blip. In fact, he spent just as much time with them as their sound engineer, though as a dance act that required less effort than it might have done for the Dare roadies. 'It was just when [singer] Peter Cunnah was essentially on his own,' he remembers. 'It was just driving him around the country in my car with a DAT (Digital Audio Tape) player. We'd drive to some club in Middlesborough, or somewhere and then he'd get his mic and sing, and I'd play the DAT player.' For this, he would receive £20 a night.

Dare fan club chief Mick Taylor recalls hearing on the

grapevine that Cox had begun road managing a new band. This wasn't strictly true. Back from Berlin, he felt right about leaving the band and heading back to academia. His time with Dare had been exciting and different, but the studious boy who once wired up his grandpa's shed was still hiding away behind the long hair and ripped jeans. Having crawled to the end of his A-levels while juggling the group, he returned to full-time education and set about rectifying that D in Maths, picking up a text book and starting to re-learn properly what he had done rather haphazardly five years previously. He decided to apply, like everyone else but a little bit older, to university. 'I knew I wanted to do physics,' he said.

Back home with his parents in Oldham, he applied to several of the top red-brick universities, including Liverpool, Edinburgh and Durham. The University of Manchester was obviously on the list. Not only was it considered one of the best universities in the country but it had a fantastic science department, especially physics. The faculty was large, it had thriving research and Jodrell Bank Observatory was affiliated to it and nearby. It also had connections with several of the foreign institutions that Cox would subsequently participate in, including the HERA collider in Hamburg (a large particle accelerator much like he would subsequently work on at CERN) and Tevatron in Chicago. He thought maybe he should move away from his hometown, spread his wings a little and see what life was like outside the Northwest, but Manchester and its staff impressed him. 'When I came to Manchester, I think it was a combination of the history of the place and Jodrell Bank was a huge draw for me because I started doing astrophysics, actually,' he said. 'And to be at the university that owned one of *the* most famous radio telescopes in the world was a big thing for me. Also, the staff I met and research that was going on at the time, back in the mid-Nineties, just really captured my imagination. So, almost against my instinct to move out of my hometown, I came to [Manchester] and I've stayed here ever since.'

He was accepted into the university – perhaps unsurprising for a local private school boy – and then had to wait for the next academic year. 'It was a bit of a change, but it just felt right,' he said. Meanwhile, money was tight and an opportunity came along. 'I needed a summer job to bridge me over until I went to university,' he recalls. 'A mate of mine had just been sound engineering for [D:Ream] and said that they were shit and he didn't want to do it anymore. So I said I'd do it because I needed a bit of cash.' That was when he met Peter Cunnah. Like Cox, Northern Ireland native Cunnah had started out in a rock band. In 1990, trying to follow in the footsteps of bands like Happy Mondays and Ride, he had decided to move to London, where he arrived with £100 in his pocket and slept on the floor of a friend. He joined another band called Baby June, although it didn't feel like they were going anywhere. But something had happened in London and that was the House scene. Cunnah was hooked, going out to clubs as often as he could and listening to a different kind of music. Two of his favourite hangouts were Love Ranch and The Brain, where a young DJ called Al Mackenzie plied his trade.

Disliking the material that Baby June were producing, Cunnah asked Mackenzie to remix it and after a session in the studio came out with three versions of songs, which convinced them both that they needed to form a band together. Thus, D:Ream was born. A record deal was still elusive, though and so Cunnah made do with the PA gigs for which he had hired Cox. However, as Cox seems to have an uncanny ability to do, he had picked a winner – or at least a band with some legs. Cunnah and Mackenzie's music began to gain traction and they scored a record deal. The first song 'U R The Best Thing' went out through a small management and record company called FXU and was released in July 1992. It reached No. 72 in the charts and was eerily similar to the Dare experience – young band, good songs, company behind them, few sales.

In the October, Cox arrived at the University Of Manchester. It was everything he had hoped for. 'I think it takes a little bit of time to work out how precious and how valuable your time at university really is,' he reflected, some 20 years later. 'Being an undergraduate is the time you learn most. For me certainly, I felt my brain was waking up. I was going to say waking up again, but actually waking for the first time, almost. Because the amount of information that's fed to you and the way it's fed to you, it's a really unique experience. For me it was more valuable, because I knew that was going to be the case because I'd chosen to come back to it. For me, what I enjoyed about studying physics at Manchester was the breadth of research that was going on in the physics department. I can't overstate the importance of that.

'If you're going to be taught about lasers, or you're going to be taught about astrophysics, particle physics, quantum mechanics, the best way to be taught is to be taught by active researchers in the field. And this is a huge advantage

Manchester physics has – of being *so* big that we have experts across pretty much every field of physics that you're going to study.' He delved into the legendary textbooks, relishing the deep thinking required. 'There are two famous physics textbooks,' he said. 'One of them is Goldstein, it's called *Classical Mechanics* and the other one's [by] Jackson and is called *Classical Electrodynamics* – anybody who's done a physics degree will know them. Jackson's book is bigger. You could just sit there for years and not understand everything. And probably decades and not do all the problems in it.'

1993 was when D:Ream finally got it right. They were taken on by Magnet Records, an ageing label which had recently been bought and revitalised by Warner Brothers. 'U R The Best Thing' had been anointed DJ Pete Tong's Essential Tune of 1992, but that hadn't seemed to help. Amazingly, when 'Things Can Only Get Better' – the song that would later catapult them to the top of the charts – was released at the end of January 1993, it only got to No. 24. But in April that year, they re-released 'U R The Best Thing' and it sneaked into the Top 20. The band were asked to appear on the BBC's *Top of the Pops*. Cunnah decided they should address their stage act. 'Doesn't it really piss you off when it's a brilliant record but all you get is someone plonking away on a keyboard with a couple of Muppet dancers flanking the stage?' he told the *NME* at the time. They needed a stage full of personnel and their sound engineer-cum-friend Brian Cox fit the bill.

Almost by accident, the university physics student was in a band again. 'They needed a keyboard player to do a television show,' said Cox. 'I just stood there and waved my hair around.'

And what mighty hair it was! With locks almost down to his waist (no mullet this time) and wearing what can only be described as a skinny sleeveless tartan-esque suit – over a bare chest, no less – Cox found himself on the most legendary pop show in British history. 'It was brilliant,' he recalled to BBC Radio 4. 'I'd never done it with Dare. We did one with the Bee Gees and one with Robert Plant, so that was iconic. It's like *The Sky at Night* actually, this thing that I'd grown up with that I could be a part of.'

It was the first of five appearances on the *Top of the Pops* show. The Bee Gees episode was particularly thrilling. Speaking to the *Sunday Mirror*, he said: 'I really wanted their autographs but didn't have any paper. The only thing I had was my physics exam syllabus, so I ripped a page out of that and got them all to sign it.' Two more singles followed, though didn't fare any better than No. 19 and then the band got two big breaks. One was a call from America to tell them 'U R The Best Thing' had gone to No. 1 in the Billboard Hot Dance Club Play chart on 17 July. They travelled to the States, where the record company put on a limo and they performed a few times in Los Angeles, but it was a call from the office of a certain Mancunian boy band that really put them on the map. At the time Take That were the UK's biggest pop group and their tour was a guaranteed chance to target thousands of young people. D:Ream were tapped as the lads' support act.

'It was a bit of a shock because we were this hip, young dance act and they were… well, they were Take That,' Cunnah told the *Guardian*. 'Clubbers only buy singles and 12-inch singles. Working with Take That meant access to a much bigger market, one where girls waved banners saying they loved you.' The group seized the opportunity to widen their fan base and ended up having a riotous time. 'In Aberdeen, our dressing rooms were caravans that the fans had to go past,' recalled Cunnah. 'Jason [Orange] and Gary [Barlow] thought it would be a good idea to clamber on top of our caravan, so they did and 200 fans ran up to it, screaming and just rocked our caravan. It was like a roar of thunder – frightening!' Cox and his band mates were beginning to revel in the spotlight, too. While in Aberdeen staying at the Thistle Hotel, they had to be asked by a member of staff to stop annoying their fellow guests by playing the piano and singing in the bar at three in the morning.

For Cox, this was a bizarre time. 'It was mental,' he said. 'I was a student, so I would be in the lab doing experiments or in lectures during the day. Then I'd take off my lab coat, get on the bus and be playing live in front of 50,000 in Manchester's G-Mex stadium in the evening.' The students he spent time with in the lab loved the fact they had a pop star in their midst, but he had to endure a lot of teasing from the other side. Unlike with his Dare band mates, who had never really known about his academic proclivities, he had to keep travelling back and forth to Manchester to ensure he kept up with his studies. 'It wasn't a bad job for a student but I didn't make very much money out of it,' he told the *Sun*. 'I'd finish a physics lecture on a Friday night, then go over the road to the Manchester Evening News Arena to play a show supporting Take That. I didn't find it that weird, but I think a lot of other students did.'

With a girlfriend now in tow, he didn't indulge in the groupies on offer, but enjoyed this time as did his parents, who supported his decision and again delighted in the fact their son was playing music. Cunnah was pleased with the new more pop and mainstream direction the band was taking. 'That was wild,' he said of the Take That tour. 'We were playing to 10,000 kids a night, who weren't pissed, weren't on one, weren't old enough to be biased about what they were listening to and who gave us a damn good chance. Have we sold out? Of course not! People just always find a hole to pick in something so I want this music to reach as many people as it can.' Not everyone in the band agreed, though. At this point, founder member Al Mackenzie decided to leave. Several news reports suggested it was because he didn't agree with the way the band were progressing, supporting boy bands, but Cunnah disagreed. 'He just hated the publicity schedule we had to do,' he said. 'He's a typical DJ – he wants to make music, not waste time being interviewed.'

Cox on the other hand didn't seem to care about the publicity, mainly because he didn't appear to partake in any of it. Despite being called a group, almost every interview featured only Peter Cunnah talking about himself and what the band were going to do next; the singer became something of a music magazine pin-up. He featured in at-home pieces and there was a tabloid spread about his birth mother tracking him down. In early 1994, coverage of the band didn't include Cox at all. 'I just did the keyboards,' he said later. 'Pete was the one who got all the attention.' Yet photos of the band in *Melody Maker* and *NME* in January and February 1994 don't feature Cox at all, just Cunnah surrounded by a cache of session musicians.

There was a reason D:Ream were so ubiquitous as they rolled into 1994. They had released their first album titled rather portentously *D:Ream On Volume 1* the previous October and it had reached No. 5 in the charts. Cox is credited as playing piano on the song 'Star', which was released as part of a double A-side single at the beginning of that month. Then in January 1994, off the back of the successful Take That tour, Magnet decided to re-release 'Things Can Only Get Better'. The anthem had been written as early as 1989 by Cunnah and his songwriting colleague, Jamie Petrie; it was a shrewd move and the song rocketed to the No. 1 spot. Despite the encroaching tide of grunge, and specifically Nirvana's second album, *Nevermind*, music journalists had a soft spot for Cox's gang. 'D:Ream are the best dance act this side of the moon and it's a crime that they're not as big as M People already with their fab dancey tunes,' wrote Leesa Daniels in *Smash Hits*. In the *Melody Maker*, Ian Gittins was just as effusive. 'With their compelling sunrise keyboard breaks and positivist mantras, [D:Ream] soon became a clubland inspiration, an underground totem,' he said.

'Things Can Only Get Better' remained in the charts for an impressive 16 weeks. Fifteen years on, a *Guardian* reader picked Cox up on the song as being a breach of the second law of thermodynamics, referring to the inevitable decay occurring in the universe as a result of entropy and how the title directly opposes this theory. Cox had a sense of humour about it. 'It is,' he replied, 'and I've already apologised for the scientific inaccuracy in this and other D:Ream songs.' In March, the group followed their success with yet another re-release for 'U R The Best Thing', which this time reached No. 4. The single's lyrics appeared in *Smash Hits'* famous songbook section and now they charged £9 a ticket for audiences to see them on tour in venues such as The Anvil in Basingstoke and the Manchester Apollo, a hall familiar to Cox from his Dare days. Every month, they'd have all-night parties at Cunnah's flat after a night out at trendy London nightspot Subterania. Pete Stanton reviewed the single in *Smash Hits*, giving it four stars and calling the keyboard sound 'plinkety pianos'.

Throughout all this, Cox was keeping up with university work, maintaining the good grades that would keep him on course to continue with his studies beyond BSc level into post-graduate status. With D:Ream about to head off on a world tour, just as he had three years before, he now faced a choice. 'I've made very few big decisions,' he explained to Kirsty Young on Radio 4's *Desert Island Discs*. 'I've sort of been carried along in life. But one of them was the second year of university when D:Ream got very big and I think we'd just toured with Take That. D:Ream went off on a big world tour to Australia, America – and so the question came up, "do you stay at university or do you go off and tour the world?"' Cox chose to quit the band and remain at Manchester, a decision he never regretted. He was tired of schlepping around the world in someone else's pocket and wanted to concentrate on using his brain. 'It was brilliant,' he said, 'but I got out at the right time.'

Just as with Dare, his departure came at the right time for the fortunes of the band. Cunnah had an escalating drugs problem and any notion of it being a collective was gone. Instead, D:Ream was only the frontman and what *Smash Hits* described as a 'floating group of musicians'. In 1995, they released second album, *World*, which didn't received such acclaim as the first and despite the single 'Shoot Me With Your Love' reaching No.

7, Cunnah broke up the band – 'I became pretty obnoxious,' he later explained in an interview.

Cox had long since gone back to focusing on physics by then, but of course this wasn't the end of his days as a D:Ream-er. In 1997, Labour looked to shatter 18 years of Conservative rule at the General Election in May. Change was the by-word on every shadow politician's lips and some bright spark in the campaign office thought it might be an idea to adopt a song reflecting that ideal. And so it was that 'Things Can Only Get Better' received yet another lease of life as the soundtrack for the wannabe new government. Cox was in Hamburg working on his PhD when he took a call from Peter Cunnah to ask if he fancied getting the band back together. He had just been awarded a first-class honours degree from Manchester and had chosen to stay on as a post-grad and further his qualifications. 'Pete rang me up and said, "Do you want to pop back on stage? It'll be a laugh,"' Cox told Shortlist. 'And it was.'

The band went on rallies up and down the country, meeting future Prime Minister Tony Blair on a number of occasions. 'It was all so surreal,' revealed Cunnah to the *Guardian*. 'I was on the Prescott Express, going round the country, performing with Tony Blair and listening to loads of fortysomethings sing my song. One day [John] Prescott told me he was fed up with the song because he'd sung it so many times. And I said, "John, don't even go there!" – I was the really fed-up one.' Still, Cox enjoyed getting back in the pop saddle. As before, his parents had been cautious when he resigned from the group, thinking it might prove a backward step. After all, the five years of previously being in Dare had formed his character, taking him from a teenager to a young adult. Up on stage with D:Ream again – and for what, at the time, felt like such a momentous cause – made him very happy. 'Being part of the election in 1997 was an iconic moment,' he said. 'We were right at the centre of the action and our song was at the heart of it.'

'Things Can Only Get Better' was released as a single for the third time at the beginning of May 1997 and got as high as number 19. On the day of the election, the band recorded an appearance on *Top of the Pops*. 'We went to a hotel Labour had got us, overlooking the Houses of Parliament,' Cox remembered to the *Observer*. '[We] sat there, watched all those classic moments. Portillo getting voted out!' With the results in, Cox and his band mates headed to the Royal Festival Hall in London for the Labour victory party. At the time of writing, it was the last time they appeared onstage. YouTube is full of videos featuring Blair and his cohorts singing along to the song. 'There's that famous scene when John Prescott, Robin Cook, Neil Kinnock and everyone were dancing,' said Cox, 'so that was my fault.' With hindsight, some people have criticised the band for being part of New Labour, but Cox himself only remembers a scene of optimism and happiness. In fact, author John O'Farrell used the song's title for his book about being a Labour supporter in opposition between 1979 and 1997.

Many years later, Cox bumped into Blair in Oxford and the two had a brief catch-up. 'I've got good memories and bad,' Cunnah told writer Nicole Veash in 2001. 'I'll never forget Peter Mandelson fluffing the words. Or the big bear hug that Alastair Campbell gave me as Portillo lost his seat. But even now I can't stand listening to the song. I'm sure Tony Blair feels the same way.'

D:Ream broke up again soon afterwards and went their separate ways. Cunnah had escaped his drug addiction by the time Labour came calling, but despite Cunnah investing £60,000 of his own money into a third studio album, record bosses weren't interested and it remained unreleased. A Best Of was unveiled instead. He moved into songwriting, penning music for an ITV kids' show called *Star Street*. Mackenzie returned to his day job as a DJ on the club circuit. Cox went back to Germany, but has since talked about the usefulness of his time as a pop star after he became a television celebrity. 'As I've got into this new career in the media, it's a good grounding,' he explained in 2011. 'The way that I handle increasing levels of attention has a lot to do with the fact I'd had to do it once, albeit in a smaller bubble. It's helped.'

He has also joked that the standard of groupie he gets nowadays is higher than when he was performing. 'More educated,' he laughed to the *Sunday Times*. 'Let's just say when they wake up in the morning, they're more likely to read the *Sunday Times* than the *News of the World*.' However, physics continued to be his primary focus. 'Being a scientist is more than just a job you do,' he said. 'It really does shape the way that you look at the world and what excites you and what interests you. It gives you the tools, I suppose, to really appreciate nature and appreciate the universe for what it is. Which is magnificent. It's a path to an excellent career, but it's a path to immense entertainment, a real box of treasures.'

Right now, that treasure box was waiting for him in Germany.

CHAPTER 5

ACADEMIA, LOVE AND TV

Brian Cox had a first-class degree and like most scientists had decided to stay on at university and pursue his PhD. By the time New Labour came calling, he was fully ensconced in the next cycle of his academic journey. Manchester had a strong post-graduate programme and his desire to spend time in the lab as a researcher was acute. 'We need first-class researchers,' he said. 'Because whilst the technology of today is based on the science of yesterday, the technology of tomorrow is going to be based on today's science and you do not know what you're going to find out about the universe.'

Though he had started out concentrating more on astrophysics and even cosmology, he now narrowed his focus as he progressed towards what he would ultimately become known for: particle physics. This was useful, because Manchester University had strong ties with the world's leading particle physics labs, home to the best particle accelerators – Tevatron in Chicago, Hamburg's HERA and CERN, where the idea of the Large Hadron Collider (the world's largest particle accelerator) was at that time in the midst of germinating. He had a season ticket to Oldham Athletic, where he watched his favourite players of the era, among them Andy Ritchie. And it was at this time that he met the man who would end up as a close friend and collaborator. Professor Jeff Forshaw – as he is now – was a very young lecturer at Manchester University when the pair first came into contact during Cox's post-graduate days. A theoretical physicist by trade, Forshaw immediately saw something in the student sitting in his class. 'He's about the same age as me, so he was a little bit different in the class,' remembers Forshaw. 'I taught a class of about 20 people and Brian was one of the students and we got talking. He being a little bit older and a little more confident to come and talk to me afterwards, we immediately hit it off. We're very good friends and we just clicked quite early on, going out drinking together, going out on runs together, from quite an early stage. Because he was doing a PhD and because we were the same age and because I was quite a young academic at the time, it wasn't like teacher/student – there wasn't that kind of formality associated with it.'

In fact, Forshaw felt Cox was a breath of fresh air, someone who had come to the scientific profession having had a full and interesting life away from it, unlike many career academics. Above all, their attitudes to science were in sync. 'What we do have in common is we do see physics in a similar way and I think that's very important in a collaboration,' he says, referring to later joint professional efforts. 'If you're not on the same wavelength as somebody else, it can be quite difficult to talk about the ideas and make progress talking about them. Brian and I do tend to think in a very similar way. And we ask questions of each other that help us to make progress in developing the understanding so in that sense we bonded on this. The friendship developed first. And always we've spent a lot of time outside of a formal physics session, just talking about physics and talking about how we see physics; how we understand concepts in physics.'

With a close friendship now formed, work on the PhD began in earnest. 'I started studying supernovas, when stars at the end of their life explode and a colossal amount of energy comes out,' he told young interviewers from Stockley School who managed to bag a chat with him at the Big Bang Fair, 'so I worked on how to detect them on earth and then I went into particle physics. I started working on the structure of the proton.' It became clear that he needed to go and work at a particle accelerator, where huge detectors studied atoms up close in a prelude to the Large Hadron Collider. The Deutches Elektronen-Synchrotron (DESY) is the largest German research centre for particle physics – a lab located in Bahrenfeld, a suburb west of Hamburg.

Founded in December 1959 and funded by public money, this was home to the Hadron-Electron Ring Accelerator (HERA), the first electron-proton collider in the world. Constructed between 1984 and 1990 (and going online in 1992), it was one of the first internationally financed projects of this scale, though it has since shut down in 2007. Like the Large Hadron

Collider at CERN, it was housed in a large tunnel (in HERA's case, 6.3km long, between 10 and 25m underground), running outside the DESY site. The H1 detector was hidden by a dark red concrete wall, which itself hid a three-storey high electronics trailer. At around 2,800 tonnes, it was monitored and run by a team of approximately 300 physicists from 15 different countries. Ostensibly a general purpose detector built to deal with the collision of leptons and protons, H1 had some specific tools, namely to study particle jets in specially-constructed chambers, silicon trackers and muon detectors. This meant it was equipped to handle jet and particle production, as well as diffraction – an area of physics that Cox was particularly interested in.

Cox began visiting the facility about three years after work began in 1995, something he continued for a number of years. 'He was not so much living in Hamburg as visiting spasmodically,' says Professor John Dainton, now the Sir James Chadwick Chair of Physics at the University Of Liverpool, but then the physics co-ordinator at HERA. 'He joined as a PhD student. PhD students would come out and spend time at the laboratory, as well as work in their home university departments. When he first came, I was just becoming what we call the physics co-ordinator of this big group of physicists, which means I was responsible for all the physics output – making sure the 300 physicists could get their papers out, properly refereed and that we were doing the physics we should do. While he was on the experiment, I was also what's called a spokesperson, which is head of the experiment.'

From Dainton and his team's point of view, HERA's goal was

extremely simple. 'Particle physics has been concerned with trying to understand the very shortest distances and times, and how it relates to physical law,' he explains. 'We've been pushing to get higher and higher energy in collisions of what are known to be the pieces of matter that we understand are basic presently. This meant we started off with colliders back in the Seventies that were 3 or 4 GeV [giga-electron volt, a unit for measuring how much energy passes through an electron] and we went right through up to 300 GeV [on HERA]. The LHC is going up to 14,000 GeV. [HERA] was the only collider that collided head-on a particle that we think we still understand, called the electron, which is one of the two particles in the hydrogen atom and the simplest atomic nucleus which is called a proton. Two rings ramped the beams up to these high energies and we built a big experiment called H1 around one of the interaction regions.

'And there was another experiment in another interaction regions. It was a smaller version of the LHC, but it was designed to use the electrons to drill holes in the proton and understand what the proton is made of – break it up in ways we could measure. And in that way we could understand what a proton is made of, and what are the laws of force that hold it together, and how these pieces called "the quarks" interact with the electron. We had a pretty good idea how an electron would interact with a quark, we hoped that idea would be wrong and what we essentially found was we could measure extremely accurately how an electron and a quark interacted and it fitted a pre-conceived picture called a standard model.'

Cox's direct supervisor was Robin Marshall, a scientist who

has since retired. He held the equivalent chair to Professor Dainton in Manchester and spent his time at the university running the group that Cox was a part of. '[Cox] was engaged in the experiment and he did his stuff,' says Dainton, who saw Brian most days in the corridor for a chat, but would remain apart from him and his drinking buddies socially. 'It's a collaborative effort, so there are certain things you have to take responsibility for if you want to be a part of it – it's a huge enterprise.' Working on a project such as the H1 meant that Cox had to lend his signature to the academic papers and reports produced, alongside all those working on it. That meant keeping to a schedule, something he wasn't always good at.

'I can remember exactly [what he was doing] because he took too long to write the paper on it,' Dainton recalls. 'I spent half my time saying "where's your paper, where's your paper?" He took a long time because he was doing all this other stuff.' Nevertheless, the physics he was doing at HERA fed nicely into his PhD thesis, which was eventually published and titled 'Rapidity Gaps Between Jets in Photo Production at HERA'. It was about a special kind of collision between photons (light particles) and protons (sub-atomic particles which help make up an atom's nucleus). 'One of the things we discovered at HERA was that the proton has a structure that we expected, but it also exhibits other aspects,' explains Dainton. 'Namely aspects which tell you why or how two protons interact with each other. We discovered a particular sort of interaction that we could measure in a certain way. It was completely unexpected. Brian worked on essentially trying to understand how this phenomena was related to the way the quarks came out of the interaction. The quarks come out and they make jets – they literally look like jets in the detector.

'Brian was working on interactions in which there were essentially two jets, but they didn't seem to talk to each other enough as they came out. They didn't get mixed up as much as they should do. We called them "diffractive jets" or "jets with a rapidity gap". He worked on a sample we had in the data we took. His thesis was on this – a theorist in Manchester helped him, called Jeff Forshaw.'

When Cox asked Forshaw to help him with his PhD paper, the latter jumped at the chance. '[He was] someone enthusiastic and very capable,' said Forshaw. And he spent a fair amount of time out in Hamburg working with Cox. 'I remember staying up all night listening to the Beatles when we had a talk to present at nine o'clock in the morning in Hamburg,' he continues. 'We were doing a double act, I think – two talks, one after the other, starting at nine o'clock. And I think we only went to bed at about six o'clock in the morning, had two hours' sleep, and went off again and gave these talks. We spent the whole night listening to the Beatles and talking physics – I remember that really vividly.'

A typical day or week at HERA could be long and tiring. Cox might be running shifts, which would involve 10 eight-hour days, then 24 hours off. This could include night shifts too, whichever run you were chosen to do. It was all about manning the experiment and keeping it going, taking the data; it would also mean examining the computer and what the data meant, attacking the data in a way that you could try to measure something specific, depending on what was being measured and in what capacity. 'He would have to give talks to the group and he'd probably have to help a few graduate students who were younger than him,' explains Dainton.

Life at DESY was much the same as in any lab. 'The lab is on a big campus, but my wife was head of what's called the International Office at the lab and her job was to get visiting scientists accommodation near to it,' adds Dainton. 'They'd have an apartment to live in, there'd be a social life around it – it was completely international.' A scientific facility isn't like most corporations, though. Everyone is working towards the same goal and if they fail, they won't necessarily be shouted at or criticised as in an average job, but they may feel shame that they haven't achieved what they set out to do. It's a drive, as Cox has subsequently suggested, towards doing something that will change the world for the better; it also means young scientists are completely cosmopolitan.

'I don't know how Brian mixed in with his peers, but he was in the international world,' says Professor Dainton. 'It must have influenced him – it would influence anyone in those circumstances. The young people like Brian who are working on the experiment, they're all working together. They don't think about where a person comes from. I've watched so many young people go through that experience in the last 25/30 years, that they come out and they stand head and shoulders above their peers, just because they know how the world works.' Dainton also points out that one thing the British students at international facilities such as HERA are taught to do is to speak slowly and with not too thick an accent. When presenting a paper to the team on the ground, it was important to remember not all of them spoke great English. Though Dainton cannot remember specifically doing that for Cox, it's not all that far-fetched to imagine that he may have learnt some of his clarity of speech from Hamburg days.

As a scientist, his co-ordinator remembers a 'run-of-the-mill student mucking in with everyone else.' Dainton adds: 'Brian has done some good things in his research, no question about it. [But] he's not going to intellectually change the world, like some of the stars in the field. I don't for a moment think Brian's going to produce the grand unified theory. I don't for a moment think that Brian's going to make the measurement that will tell us whether neutrinos do travel faster than the speed of light – I don't think he's that sort of physicist. I think he can describe what he's doing to a layman in his own style, which obviously appeals to the people he talks to.'

While fairly anonymous from a professional point of view, Cox was beginning to show signs of his subsequent interest in the media when he returned to HERA after finishing his thesis in a post-doctoral capacity, emboldened and more confident. 'He was obviously a more mature student because his background was telling us things were going to get better,' says Dainton. 'At the time, he was very media-savvy, there's no question about that – in the sense that he was aware of the media all the time and he was always interested in talking to people outside the field. But as time went on, he was obviously getting more and more interested in the media because I remember one time he rolled up on a Thursday, which is when we had the group meeting. And in the morning, I was just about to go to the group meeting and literally half an hour before, he rolled up with recording equipment and said he'd just come in from the UK and he wanted to record the group meeting because he was doing a Radio 4 programme. I kind of looked at him and said, "So, you're just going to roll up with that, are you?" and he said yes. So I said, "Well, wait a minute – I think we're going to have to ask the group" – and I think there were about 100 people in this meeting – "whether they mind being recorded and if they say yes, we can do it, but you should first of all ask them." So, he was already into it at that stage, in 1998/99 or something.'

More than a decade on and Dainton is slightly shocked at how the wannabe radio presenter has taken over television. 'Last time I saw him for any length of time was at the 350th anniversary celebration of the Royal Society. He saw me, and came over and chatted, and after about four sentences he was surrounded by these 17- or 18-year-old schoolgirls who wanted his autograph. And I thought, my God, he's become a celebrity!'

Dainton is aware of the potential pitfalls of trying to balance a media career with being a professional scientist, though. 'You can see it already – and this is nothing against him because I rather like him – [but] if he continues to go down this route, he's going to be a celebrity and if that's what he wants, then the very best of luck to him. But celebrities exist in a kind of bubble and suddenly if the public decides to turn against them, the bubble bursts. Science is not like that: science is something that you don't have a bubble. You start off standing on your own little rock, claiming and doing what you're trying to do because you're committed to it, and you end up – with a bit of luck – actually adding to that rock in a systematic way in terms of the body of knowledge and understanding which leaves you feeling okay, ten, fifteen, twenty years later. You've not earned pots of money, you've had a reasonable salary, you feel you contributed a lot; it's long, hard graft.

'It seems to me he has to make the judgment about what he wants and I personally, like a lot of scientists, would step back and say "We can't help you with creating a media bubble, it's not in the nature of what we do." Stardom, though is a different kind of achievement and one that's not necessarily compatible with that life.

'This is all beginning to sound a bit too much like hyping a personality,' Dainton continues. 'I think what he's done is he's landed on his feet doing what he's good at. The media are hyping him at the moment. They're hyping him because he appeals to teenagers and to mums and dads, who see their teenagers doing things that are motivated by something they think is worthwhile – he clicks, he's not stuffy. There's a great danger here you're creating a super-character out of someone I regard as perfectly normal. I totally support him [trying to convey science to the general public], just as I think that it's absolutely wonderful that Bruce Forsyth at the age of 80-plus can still dance around and make people happier because he can make them dance. But Bruce Forsyth is doing it as well for another reason – it gives him a bloody good living and he's a celebrity. And Brian's the same. He's doing it for a bloody good living and the very best of luck to him! The fact that he also helps me in getting good students is a bonus for me, so I tend to go a bit more for Brian than I do for Bruce Forsyth.'

Not everyone in the scientific community is quite so open-minded, though. Just as bringing a recording device into a

HERA meeting caused some distress, so Dainton suggests the transition of an academic into the public arena – and his acceptance there – is bound to cause some jealousy. 'This is not my opinion, but I can understand it,' he argues. 'Brian is a particle physicist by training. However, I went to the Royal Society and I was sitting next door having lunch with a senior colleague and on my other side was an astronomer, who was on a committee I was on from Manchester. My colleague lent across the table and said to this astronomer, "So when Mr Cox finishes his Royal Society Fellowship, are you going to have him back in Manchester?" And the astronomer was looking venomous at the mention of the word "Cox" and just said, "Oh sure, when he comes back, he's going to get a huge, full teaching load. Blah, blah, blah, blah…" And the way he said it, said it all.

'Many astronomers would professionally react to a person like Brian talking about astronomy and I can understand them thinking that way. I don't – I don't mind him at all talking about astronomy or particle physics. But there are people in science who would take a rather, shall we say, religious view of how you do what Brian does and would not feel happy about somebody who's not Patrick Moore talking about astronomy. And Brian isn't an astronomer.

'I think that's rather a pathetic point of view but nevertheless, it must be something Brian has to deal with. And I don't know what's happened – I don't know whether he's gone back to Manchester at all, whether he's permanently employed on the BBC. You can see that reflects a perspective, which is understandable in the circumstances by people working in the same department. There's bound to be, shall we say, odd reaction in the sense of envy maybe, I don't know.'

Nevertheless, Professor Dainton admits: 'We all know that Brian Cox works at his image – people who are in the media do that sort of thing. [Brian's] serving an audience he's picked out. I'm sure he's recognised this himself. It's the 13- and 14-year-olds and their mums and dads. Whereas Jim Al-Khalili would be on BBC4 and BBC2, Brian would be much more BBC1-ish, if you see what I mean. He's doing things in the media that are taking him in a particular direction. He's been on *QI*, he's been on some of those late night comedy shows – he's going that way. Marcus du Sautoy isn't, nor is Jim Al-Khalili, [but] anybody who helps to explain to the taxpayer – who's my paymaster – why their money is being spent well, is doing a very good job. And there's absolutely no doubt that all the people who do that, including Brian, know very well that the British taxpayer's investment in science is spent extremely efficiently.

'I have no more or no less respect for him than I have for some of the most introverted but brilliant physicists I'm lucky to work with. I haven't spoken to him for two or three months. He's having to make a choice whether he goes with the media stuff or with the science because to stay in the science it's very tough, it's very competitive. He used to keep saying to me, "I'm going to get back into physics now," after his first series on the Solar System. Then along came the second series. And he hasn't popped up on his experiment, I believe, at the LHC for some time. I think there is a great danger that these things can roll out of control and then the bubble bursts.'

The thing is, Cox was happy to combine his academic work

with some dabbling in the media by the turn of the 21st century. Hong Kong entrepreneur Richard Li, the son of his country's then-richest man, had an audacious plan to converge the internet and television as never before. Network of the World was the result – a series of five web portals and an Asian satellite TV channel based in west London, employing 400 staff. Launched with great pomp in June 2000, one of those portals was called Earth & Space and it needed content. An aspiring young scientist fitted the bill.

And so did Gia Milinovich, an American ex-pat who had been in England since 1987 after leaving her hometown of Duluth, Minnesota. A sassy, pretty, clever young woman, she had grown up putting on her own TV shows with her sister, dreaming of being a nightclub singer, doctor or cheerleader. 'When I think back to my childhood, I realise that though my mother thought I was just a lazy sod, my obsession with watching television was actually research,' she said. 'I never sang pop songs into my hairbrush, I always played TV presenter. Sometimes I was the host of a music programme or an entertainment programme or was often the reporter interviewing my mother, my friends or my sister, who were playing various roles. I'd write the scripts, the jingles, the ads even and direct everyone – even telling them exactly what to say in response to my questions.'

Her grandparents were close friends of Bob Dylan's parents in Minnesota and Beatty Zimmerman (Dylan's actual surname) was the first person to dress up as Father Christmas for her. By the time she finished high school, Milinovich wanted to be an actress or a journalist, having edited her school newspaper. 'In the end I decided to study acting,' she said. She enrolled in theatre arts at the University of Minnesota, grappling with the Method style by pretending to eat non-existent lemons and drinking cups of imaginary coffee. 'After a couple of years I realised that I wasn't really hungry enough and was never going to earn the kind of living I wanted out of acting. About two weeks after I decided to pack in the acting, I went for an open audition for presenters for a new teenage entertainment programme. Out of almost 1,000 people, I ended up getting the job.'

That was 1992 and the job was a show with Gareth Jones, otherwise known as kids' host, 'Gaz Top'. Excited but petrified, she realised she had a problem. 'I knocked on Gareth's door, went in, told him that I had no idea how to present a live, unscripted programme and that I really needed help,' she revealed. 'He spent the next fifteen minutes telling me everything I ever needed to know about presenting. He's my best friend to this day.' Several jobs immediately fell into her lap before the inevitable lull, including Nickelodeon's *Hot or Not?* and *Ice Warriors* on Sky Sports. In her downtime, she worked behind the scenes as an assistant producer and director. 'In 1994, I was asked to write a piece on technology for a BBC Radio 5 computer, technology and internet programme called *The Big Byte* as a kind of audition piece,' she remembered. 'The producer liked it and hired me as computer culture correspondent. I didn't really know much about the internet or computers at all – I had had a ZX-81 when I was a kid and messed around on the nascent Net with friends as a teenager, but I certainly wasn't a geek.'

She had a chance to remedy this when she became pregnant

in the mid-1990s. Son Moki was born and in the aftermath of his birth, she decided to specialise as a science and technology presenter. 'When my baby son was sleeping, I'd devour general science books on physics and astronomy,' she said. 'I taught myself Photoshop and HTML coding, I got online and learned everything I could about it.' Her perseverance was rewarded on going back to work. In 1999, she was hired to present *The Kit* on BBC Knowledge and soon became established as a tech expert. She also began to take a deeper role in the content and make-up of the shows she participated in, preferring the job title 'broadcast journalist' to 'TV presenter'.

'Ideally, I'd like to write, produce, present, direct, edit, commission and hand myself a BAFTA!' she joked. 'I have a lot to say about a lot of things and though I'm happy doing the odd day here and there of just "stand there, say that" presenting, I am most happy when I can take an active role in programme-making. I'm not very good at sitting around and hoping that someone else will come up with an idea for a programme that I'd be interested in working on and offer me a job, so I just started doing it myself. I've always felt that my role as a presenter has been to impart information and producing is the natural step for me to take.'

She broke up with Moki's father just as their son was about to start primary school. Because he suffers from dysgraphia (the writing equivalent of dyslexia, which was only officially diagnosed when he was 13), Moki always needed extra attention in school and was privately educated, paid for by his father. Milinovich's deal was that she would eschew maintenance in exchange for this. But single motherhood in London was tough and there were times when they had very little money. By the time Moki came along, Milinovich had been a vegetarian for 10 years after signing to The Smiths' message on their *Meat Is Murder* album. She fed him a varied diet, including some Japanese and Eritrean dishes, but stayed away from junk food (though they later started eating meat as a family).

Having grown up in a house with a sister and parents who discussed political issues and watched the news every night, she did the same with Moki, debating topics and making fun of George W. Bush. In fact, by the time he started school and was hearing swearing around the playground, she initiated a rule at home whereby the only time he was allowed to swear was when he was talking about the then-President. In fact, he *had* to. Despite the fact she, too is a self-confessed atheist and rationalist, she excitedly told him about the Easter Bunny, Santa Claus and even played Tooth Fairy when he started to lose his baby teeth.

On the work front, Network of the World sounded exciting. There was money behind it, the proprietors were ambitious and were looking to enter a market that had so far remained untapped. The company, as it turned out, was completely ahead of its time. 'I still believe Network of the World was an amazing idea. Network of the World was a real pioneer of multimedia TV,' argues Chiara Bellati, now a series producer/director of large-scale science shows, but back then the producer/director for the Earth & Space and Tech portals. 'They managed to curate a lot of raw talent – it was really fun place to work. You hear about places like Google, where people have basketballs and chocolate in the office – that was Network of the World. When it first started going, it literally was a footie table in the corner and people coming round with chocolate bars for free.'

It was set up in conjunction with TV company Trans World International (TWI), the production arm of marketing behemoth IMG and based at their studios in Chiswick, where the British-based portion of the unit's content was generated. 'It was one of the world's first broadband-delivered television projects,' says Amanda Groom, the network's head of content. 'It involved a number of different channels and portals, six of them. The idea was you would have the linear programming, which you would have in a video player on your computer screen, whilst simultaneously relevant web pages would be available, additional supportive information would be available at the same time. It was the beginning of the multi-screen experience. I still see things today that people are describing as being absolutely cutting-edge and innovative and I think to myself, actually we were doing that a decade ago. Working there was experimental and a lot of fun.'

Part of the issue with the channels was that they were delivered via broadband and broadband had yet to be embraced by, and manufactured properly in Europe. 'We found it very difficult to show what was happening because [the audience] couldn't see it,' says Groom. 'Southeast Asia was much more advanced in terms of broadband and of course one of the powerhouses behind the project was a company called PCCW, based out of Hong Kong. So when I say it was much too early, that was its problem. It was state-of-the-art in Asia, but it was premature for the rest of the world. It worked also on the idea that if you provide the free content, you will begin to form your audience and then they'll be happy to pay for it. And that's still somewhat debated today.'

By the time Groom arrived early in the process to take on her role overseeing all the video and web output, Cox was already ensconced as part of the team. 'It was pretty much full-time,' she says of his job. 'Everyone was full-time because if you weren't actually on camera, you were back at your desk doing the supporting webpages and doing phone interviews, so it was very much a hands-on producer/presenter role. It wasn't a "let's roll out the host and tell him or her what to say", it was very much that the experts within their fields who were constantly into the work then presented the shows. It was the beginning of the current trend, which is presenters who are experts in their field; this was that idea. You were brilliant or very good in your field and then part of your job was to present the show.'

She remembers seeing Cox at his desk early every morning, preparing for what he was going to talk about on his show. 'He would do interviews, discussion, general presenting to camera around all the topics relating to earth and space,' she explains. 'Obviously space is very much his area, but we also had programming on everything from great whales of the ocean to the movements of the planets, to mountains and so forth.' Bellati also brought him in as a pundit for the Tech strand, the portal presented by Gia Milinovich. 'Brian is just a maelstrom of ideas,' says Bellati. 'He didn't necessarily get involved in the nitty-gritty of the organisational side of it or of writing scripts so much, though I think he did do some writing now and then. He was definitely a powerhouse of ideas. It was a very collaborative process. He'd come in and just suggest things, put his thinking cap on, or come in and say, "I read this, this might be interesting". So it wasn't about Brian coming in, reading a script and walking out again; it was very much Brian being involved, being excited and I know it's in retrospect, but I can tell you at the time it was a real pleasure working with him because there just wasn't a big ego there. There was just someone who was genuinely excited and genuinely very grateful for the opportunity to be doing what he was doing. He didn't take himself too seriously.'

Despite having to talk knowledgeably about subjects such as natural history that weren't part of his academic background – although one of the topics he was excited about and spent a lot of time investigating was private space travel – Cox seemed on his game. 'I don't think he was nervous at all, he was just lovely Brian!' reveals Groom. 'When I see him now I just think that's exactly who he is: relaxed, easy, friendly, nice guy. He was brilliant clearly, and he was always very easy and very nice to work with.' Once in the studio, Cox either presented solo, or with colleagues like Jane Farnham and Richard Wiese, both professional hosts. 'It was a very interesting virtual studio,' recalls Groom. 'It had extraordinary capabilities to do virtual set-ups. There were some severe limitations about camera moves and lighting, and of course there was no time between programmes because we would actually record four hours as live TV, daily. So there was no time to set up the studio differently or with any great variety, which was frustrating.

'Obviously, in the studio there was always a producer on the shows and of course a studio director, so in terms of the shows there was not so much a guiding hand, but there was back-up.

It wasn't as if he was out on his own. But in terms of the content that went into his discussion, he would have been the brains behind that always. Because he understood more than anybody else! I trusted him and I knew that he knew his stuff. There was never any question of having to breathe down his neck over supervising; there was never an issue of whether he would deliver. He was very professional, that was just Brian. It was like, "Well, if Brian wants to do it, he'll know what he's doing".' The content was topical, but aware of its potentially global audience – they were not able to react directly to breaking news. Nevertheless, the format 'let you make mistakes, which every presenter needs.' And it gave Cox a chance to bed in on camera.

'It was a nursery slope for a number of presenters but having said that, if Brian was nervous, it didn't show and there was also something comforting that so few people across Europe were watching,' says Groom. 'In fact, it had quite a big audience in Asia.' Chiara Bellati remembers a confident on-camera presence, despite being new to the game. 'I'd say that what Brian did really well with was Brian wasn't afraid,' she says. 'Sometimes with new presenters when there's an autocue, they get nervous and you get quite a stilted performance. What Brian showed, and the reason he impressed me so much, is that he didn't get stilted. Most of all he talked to the public through the camera, he didn't read to the public. In interview situations for Tech, for example, sometimes we brought him in as an expert; he'd start going off on a tangent. He'd suddenly realise, but instead of getting kerfuffled and losing the plot like so many people do, he laughed it off and laughed at himself and laughed with the public, before taking it back to the point. He had a very natural confidence and ability to go, "This is me, take me as I am," that really shone through. [The mistakes] didn't faze him the way they do many young presenters because he had the self-confidence to go, "Hey, this is fun, isn't it?!" He took it seriously in terms of enthusiasm and knowledge, but he never took himself too seriously.'

The 15-minute programmes, which went out on as a box on PC screens, changed every 15 minutes, so they were like snippets of shows. 'Because it was broadband, it was viewable with an early version of what we would now consider on demand,' explains Groom. 'There was a fairly complex set-up between satellite and broadband, and there was lots of video that was entirely on demand. You couldn't say that there were certain hours it was available, though the audience could dip into the linear programming as they saw fit.'

The core of Cox's presenting style doesn't seem to have changed much from those days just off the Hogarth roundabout in London. 'At the end of the day, Brian had already been a celebrity,' explains Bellati. 'He'd already tasted what celebrity was like through D:Ream. And the nice thing about him is he said, "How cool is this? I got to be a pop star, and now I'm on telly and I get to do physics!" And it was just that sense of "I don't know how this happened to me but it's so cool I'm really enjoying it, and I'm going to really enjoy this ride and I'm going to make the best of this ride".'

Having subsequently worked with a lot of academics, she can pinpoint the difference between them and a television natural like Cox. 'The thing with Brian is he didn't bring any attitude with his academia,' she explains. 'The things that excited him and the things he wanted to share were not from an academic's point of view. There's a lot of academics that forget the basics of what make people excited about science – they get lost in the details and the complexities. Brian had a real knack for finding the really basic things, the really simple things that still captured the public's imagination. The sort of things that still make us go, oh my God! I didn't realise that, how is that possible? Or getting something we all know and making us realise it is quite incredible. It's almost a childlike enthusiasm. Not in the sense of naïve, but in the sense of realising what is amazing about the world out there. That's what I've always carried with me about Brian, that he had this ability to see things in the same way a child would see them and appreciate them, while having a very deep understanding of them.'

Sadly, the enterprise ran out of steam pretty fast. By October 2000 – just four months after the launch – it was announced that it would be cutting back its London service. By January 2002, the UK side of the project had all but ended. 'It existed about 18 months,' says Groom. 'It then trailed on with one of the portals, which was Gamer, about gaming. That continued on for longer.' Bellati blames over-ambition. 'It changed, the money started disappearing,' she says. 'They tried to do too much, too quickly.'

Working at the company forged the kind of friendships that last a lifetime, even if it is just the occasional communication, or offer of a job, though. 'After I left Network of the World, I was still in touch with him and I actually put him forward for a couple of other series when I was at other companies,' reveals Bellati. 'There's not a lot of presenters I've pushed the way I pushed

Brian. I have a lot of time for him. This was to do with Discovery and *National Geographic*. It was a company not in the UK and they decided they wanted an American presenter. It was their loss. Nothing ever came of that, much to my disappointment.'

Bellati hasn't seen Cox in several years, but recalls a heart-warming experience after a tentpole film she worked on in 2009 reached television screens. 'I was really impressed because I did a film that came out on BBC2, part of a series for the natural history unit called *South Pacific*,' she recalls. 'I was amazed because literally two days after the film came out, I got an email from Brian saying, "Saw your film, absolutely loved it. It was amazing, love to work with you." It turned out that he was working on *Wonders of the Solar System*. He said, "I've got a series happening," and then tried to get me in touch with the exec but they'd already employed the people they needed.'

Cox waited out the demise of Network of the World, but the end of the company he called 'this bizarre thing' around him was secondary to the fact that he met the young woman who would eventually become his wife and mother to his child. When she met him, Cox was still 'wearing "student" T-shirts, spent hours playing Risk with friends and still had a single bed. He had the most horrible taste in clothes.' He thought she was pretty when he saw her on screen, but she was disappointed that the channel had hired someone from a pop band. 'The way she tells it is that she only talked to me because she thought I might help her get a bigger budget for her show,' he told the *Daily Mail*. 'Then she saw that my email address was from CERN. She is a geek herself, so she was like, "Oh wow. Maybe you're not so mindless after all."'

Gia Milinovich wasn't at all impressed by Cox's cool music background: 'When I found out, I didn't really care,' she admitted. 'All that stuff didn't really matter to me. I know loads of people in bands, it doesn't really impress me.' She thought he was a 'massive nerd', but added: 'What mattered to me were the conversations we had, the things we were writing together.' One of those projects was *Apollo's Children*, a proposal for a TV series that has never happened in the incarnation they envisaged, but now intriguingly is the name of Cox's personal website.

'When I was at Tech, I remember him putting together the first version of *Apollo's Children*,' says Bellati. '[It] wasn't *Wonders of the Universe*, but there were some elements that I recognised later on seeing *Wonders*. It made me realise there was a seed of that in *Apollo's Children*, which was his and Gia's original proposal, years and years and years ago. I thought then that it was visionary. I'm talking about a treatment I saw almost 10 years ago but I remember at the time thinking Brian is really capable of thinking big and he's right, because they're the stories that really need to be told. For him it was about getting people excited about exploring space. From what I remember, as well as a lot of the *Wonders of the Universe*-type stuff, there was a lot of what man had done to achieve the things he had done.

'I knew at the time it was a very ambitious project, in the sense I knew it would be difficult to get someone to commit that kind of money, but the BBC did the right thing backing Brian. There's not that many presenters that I was confident were going to be real stars, as I knew that Brian would be.'

Cox and Milinovich gradually got to know each other, but it wasn't until some months later that he plucked up the courage to ask her out. 'Gia says she thought I was gay when we first met and therefore she could have a non-threatening night out with me,' he says. Groom admits not realising the couple had fallen for each other. 'I don't think I was aware of it,' she says. 'There were about 200 people there. I'm sure there were a number of relationships that were starting or finishing, but I wasn't aware of that sort of side of it. I spent most of my day running from one end of the office to the other. There was a lot of fire-fighting going on, hence I didn't really notice when their relationship started.'

Bellati, however, remembers the blossoming love story. 'It was clear the two of them got on really well,' she says. 'They had a lot in common. I remember very clearly Brian saying to me how wonderful Gia was and how completely smitten he was. I remember even the night when they were at the pub and got talking. I remember Brian being completely besotted with Gia – it was really lovely.'

Cox and Milinovich arranged a date up in Manchester because he had had to go back to work at the university. She travelled up to see him on 11 September 2001. 'It was while she was on her way that the Twin Towers collapsed,' he remembered to the *Daily Telegraph*. They immediately spent the journey on the phone. 'We were both stunned – we both had a lot of friends in New York. So, on our first date we sat in and watched CNN. It was a very bonding day.' They soon became inseparable. He revelled in her geekdom. 'Any woman who collects *Star Wars* toys is fine by me,' he said. In turn, she encouraged him to wear more stylish clothes, coached him in his presenting and helped him change his image.

Both had the same view about science, which is that it needed to become part of the fabric of everyday life. 'We wanted to make science part of popular culture,' she explained. 'That was like our one-sentence manifesto and it's not about me, it's not about him, it's not about our egos: it's actually about a much bigger picture. And there was a very obvious point when I just thought, okay, I need to think about that and how are we going to do that?' This shared vision became the basis of the *Wonders* series and his subsequent outreach work. Though it didn't set the world on fire (and no footage from the portals appear to exist on the internet today), Network of the World proved invaluable for Cox's later television triumphs.

'He hasn't just fallen into this thing,' said Milinovich in 2011. 'It's been a long time of hard work. The path he took to get where he is right now has been long and slow and there have been some deliberate decisions, I suppose, made. But TV on the whole, they don't just throw someone on TV and give them a big series and send them all over the world – I mean, he's been doing TV for 10 years. That's why he's been lucky as well. We were working at a broadcaster based in London, but broadcast out in Asia, so we had huge amounts of doing live TV programmes and things like that, and no one saw it. You get incredibly valuable experience from something like that and no one sees the mistakes that you've made. He's done loads and loads and loads of things that really not that many people have seen and he suddenly pops up and it looks like he's come out of nowhere when actually it's been 10 years of hard work, running concurrently with all of his research as well.'

Chiara Bellati thinks Cox was always going to be a success on television and she could tell this, back in 2001. 'He is very driven and clear about his ideas,' she says. 'He was creative, spontaneous. He had a very easy smile and a contagious smile.' She remembers her favourite Cox moment from Network of the World: 'I can't remember what the subject matter was, but it was an interview he did with Gia and Mark Eddo, who were the presenters of Tech. We got Brian in to talk about something. Just with enthusiasm and excitement he started going down a completely different tangent. Started talking about stuff that made you want to go, "Brian, what planet are you on?" Then he looked at Gia and she obviously gave him this look and he just turned around and said, "Aargh! I've completely gone down the wrong route!" and just started laughing at himself. It was just such a spontaneous and insightful moment.'

She compares him to Leonard of Quirm, a character created by the author Terry Pratchett in his Discworld novels. Considered to be based on a mix of Leonardo da Vinci and kooky electricity pioneer Nikola Tesla, he's a great inventor and engineer, with a touch of mad genius about him. 'Sometimes Brian reminded me of that,' laughs Bellati. 'He'd be talking about something and suddenly something else would occur to him that was really exciting and off he'd go, but with a real self-knowledge of that and an ability to bring himself back. Whatever he had decided to do, he would have been a star in the making.'

Cox had met his soul mate, but he had also taken on a great

responsibility as stepfather to her young son. They got on well, but it was an adjustment to his life, which now included birthday parties at the ice rink, vomit on the white living-room rug and competitions to see who could do the most household chores. They maintained two houses: Cox in Manchester and Milinovich in London. It was frenetic, but exciting. Work was exciting, too. In October 2001, he won a prestigious Advanced Fellowship from the Particle Physics and Astronomy Research Council (PPARC), a five-year-long award aimed at those who had done one or two post-doctoral positions and were moving into proper academia. More than 250 applications were received every year and only 12 were handed out, paying his salary, some subsistence and potentially offering funding for research.

It was the next stage in what was to be an increasingly successful career, both on-screen and off. With a serious girlfriend, stepson and fellowship in tow, Cox was ready to take it to the next level.

CHAPTER 6

CERN... AND MORE

I t seems a long way from Oldham to the French Conseil Européen pour la Recherche Nucléaire, but by 2003 Brian Cox was a well-travelled man. The European Organisation for Nuclear Research, better known as CERN, was the pinnacle for any particle physicist looking to take the next step in his or her career. Established officially in 1954 and sitting astride the Franco-Swiss border near Geneva, CERN was set up as the base of a world-class fundamental physics research institute with a goal to progressing and if possible, revolutionising their branch of science. They did that and more. In 1957, they built their first accelerator (the SC) and in 1959, the Proton Synchotron (PS) became for a short time the world's most powerful particle accelerator.

Future Nobel Prize winner Georges Charpak developed the multiwire proportional chamber, which was to forever alter the way scientists were able to detect particle collisions in 1968. Then, in 1989, the Large Electron-Positron (LEP) collider was commissioned. With a circumference of 27 kilometres, the building of the tunnel alone took three years and was Europe's largest civil engineering project prior to the Channel Tunnel. The LEP was used for 11 years and provided crucial research into so-called Z particles, as well as proving definitively there are only three generations of matter. But perhaps the most incredible discovery at CERN prior to 2008 was the internet. The Web's founder, English scientist Tim Berners-Lee, created the building blocks of the net in 1989/90 while at CERN before putting it into the public domain. It was a magnanimous gesture that symbolised the ethos of the organisation – changing our lives through science and discovery for the sake of bettering humanity and nothing more. Said Cox: 'Who would have thought that a particle physics laboratory would have invented the thing that would revolutionise e-commerce and has probably generated trillions for the economy?'

The formulation for the Large Hadron Collider (LHC) began back in the early 1980s. Determined to move particle physics forward, scientists at CERN met to discuss building the biggest-ever accelerator. It wasn't until 1994 that the project was approved. ATLAS, one of the main experiments at the LHC, was approved in 1996. Established to discover the elusive Higgs boson, which would explain how particles get their mass, it was also hoped that it would explore the origins and properties of so-called dark matter. The scientific consensus is that 96 per cent of the universe is invisible in the sense that it is made up of dark matter. Initially, it was thought ALTAS might examine the existence of extra dimensions in our universe. What is a collider? In the case of the LHC (and most similar machines), it's a combination of an accelerator and detector. Explains CERN itself: 'Accelerators boost beams of particles to high energies before they are made to collide with each other or with stationary targets. Detectors observe and record the results of these collisions.'

The LHC was built in order to recreate the conditions just after the Big Bang. 'Two beams of subatomic particles called "hadrons" – either protons or lead ions – travel in opposite directions inside the circular accelerator, gaining energy with every lap,' says CERN. 'Only experimental data using the high energies reached by the LHC can push knowledge forward, challenging those who seek confirmation of established knowledge and those who dare to dream beyond the paradigm.' Cox himself summed it up: 'The thing about the LHC is that it is a new energy regime, so anything that we see is interesting.' Talking to interviewer Alan Franks, he put the new accelerator in its scientific context: 'Particle physics is often misunderstood because it is seen as being a search for new particles, whereas what you really want to know is what these particles do when they collide – basically, how the universe was built at those energies. It's not a matter of going up to high energy for the sake of it; what we have found over the 100 years since Ernest Rutherford (father of nuclear physics and professor at Manchester in 1907) is that the universe looks simpler as you get to higher energies so you are gradually uncovering the underlying structure. We know exactly the point at which our understanding fails and that point is at 10 times less energy than the LHC has got. We know that something interesting happens there and we know that it is related to mass.'

For Cox, working for CERN seemed like the natural next step. Already he had visited the facility a number of times. He had worked on the HERA project in Hamburg and more recently worked at the Tevatron collider at Fermilab in Chicago. Before it shut down in September 2011, Tevatron was the second most powerful accelerator in the world, charging beams to 99.999954 per cent the speed of light in a tunnel 4 miles in circumference, buried 25 feet underground in a campus near the city of Chicago. There, he busied himself with continuing his research, writing academic papers and giving talks. In November 1999, he was one of the presenters (along with Manchester University colleague and friend Professor Jeff Forshaw) of 'Is BFKL Ruled Out By the Tevatron Gaps Between Jets Data?' at a meeting in Batavia, Illinois. The following April, he co-wrote 'Hard Color Singlet Exchange at the Tevatron' and then in the December, he contributed to 'Diffractive Vector Boson Production at the Tevatron'.

He was doing exactly what he wanted to do – working on nuts and bolts science in one of the most prestigious labs in the world. But Manchester and its well-regarded physics department had been one of the universities that contributed to building the ATLAS detector at CERN. Building work at the LHC had been pushing on and in November 2003, ATLAS stepped into the colossal LHC structure with the installation of 18 huge feet, each 5 metres high, which were made to support the 6,000 tonne detector itself. Despite meaning he would have to move away from Gia and Moki, the family agreed it was the best career step and so Cox was off to Geneva.

Despite working at some of the most impressive particle accelerator labs in the world, nothing could prepare him for the LHC, even though it was still in the building stages. Comparing it to HERA, which he had worked on as a post-grad, demonstrates its magnitude. While HERA energised its particles to 300 GeV, the LHC could push them to around 14,000 GeV. Sitting in a tunnel almost 27 kilometres in circumference and between 50 and 175 metres underground, it was a spectacular piece of engineering and a mouth-watering enterprise for any physicist. ATLAS itself is the detector, half as big as Notre Dame Cathedral and weighing the same as 100 jumbo jets. Though it wasn't this number when Cox arrived at CERN, by December 2009, there were 2,900 scientists working on the project from 37 different countries. A section of ATLAS was tested for the first time using beams from the Super Proton Synchotron (SPS), another accelerator.

Cox ploughed straight into the work. In June 2004, he gave a talk in East Lansing, Michigan titled 'A Review of Forward Proton Tagging at 420m at the LHC and Relevant Results From the Tevatron and HERA'. Two months later, he was in Hanoi, Vietnam to speak to the 5th Recontres du Vietnam on Particle Physics and Astrophysics. Relishing the new challenge, he presented the paper 'Double Proton Tagging at the LHC as a Means to Discover New Physics'. 'I think CERN is, in my opinion, the first *Apollo* program of the 21st century in a way,' he told Oreilly.com. 'I mean, it's certainly the biggest scientific experiment ever attempted and it's journeying into the unknown in a way we haven't done for many decades in fundamental physics, in particle physics. There are some very big questions about our model of the way the universe began and how it evolved. We really are wonderfully baffled at the moment, I think it would be fair to say about the building blocks of the universe and the way the universe began and how it evolved, and the LHC is the frontier at the moment in that research.'

He loved working there. 'It's an odd job – a fantastic job, actually,' he told the *Sunday Times*. 'Your job description is to, "find out how the universe works – and here's this six billion Euro machine that you can use to do it."' For several years, he ran an upgrade project there called FP420, which was designed to result in additional particle detectors being installed close to the LHC beams. He used some of the most advanced computer programs in the world, writing simulation programs in FORTRAN, a computer language described as 'procedural, imperative, that is especially suited to numeric computation and scientific computing'. In addition, he utilised C++, a computer code that is 'statically typed, freeform and multi-paradigm'. It's safe to say he was dealing with complex levels of computer science. 'My program is a program called POMWIG, which is a derivative of HERWIG, which is one of the big Monte Carlo physics simulation programs,' he told interviewer Timothy O'Brien. He might find that harder to explain clearly to people on television.

Having worked in labs before as well as foreign countries, he soon got into the swing of things. Staying at a Holiday Inn at the foot of the Jura Mountains in France, he had to walk 20 minutes to work through the small French village of Saint-Genis. Every day, after waking up to an international newspaper and a continental breakfast of coffee, bacon baguette and pain au chocolat, he crossed the border into Switzerland with the looming peak of Mont Blanc as his backdrop. Going through the security gates, he made his way up the aptly named driveway, Route de Albert Einstein. Cox has described CERN as being an 'almost utopian village', where the higher-ups are given diplomatic licence plates for their cars. It's a busy complex – every time there's a new project (and CERN has been in existence for more than half a century so there have been plenty), a new office springs up, connected to the rest of the lab via wood-panelled corridors. It probably reminded him of school.

The sheer size and labyrinthine nature of CERN meant he still occasionally became lost on his way to the place he was working. Arriving at a white warehouse, he would descend into the LHC tunnel. As ATLAS began to take shape, it looked more and more like a spacecraft to the excited scientist, who said: 'The gleaming gold wheels at each end look like the solar panels from a giant Mars rover.' Being partly housed in France, it's unsurprising a lot of the work done at CERN is carried out in the canteen. 'Lunch is at 12,' said Cox. 'It's a bit of a race. If you go at 12.10, the canteen is packed with thousands of physicists. There's a lot of mingling – it's legendary for that. It's full of people talking about physics. They have brilliant cakes, really great elaborate things with cream and chocolate.'

And after lunch, it wasn't long before the booze came out. 'They start serving alcohol around 3 in the canteen, so people start drinking a little bit of red wine, getting more energetic and chatty,' he revealed to writer Charlotte Hunt-Grubbe. 'The trick with this kind of project is to think out of the box.' Just as in

Hamburg, where his evenings were spent shooting the breeze with Jeff Forshaw or out and about with other young members of the team, evenings often involved more animated banter over a few beers and possible a nice bottle of Châteauneuf-du-Pape. Stopping work briefly at 7pm, some alcohol would be consumed before a bit more work and then it was off to dinner. One of Cox's favourite places was the Coq Rouge, a small place in Saint-Genis. The camaraderie demonstrated just how everyone shared a common purpose. As Professor John Dainton, his supervisor at HERA explained, scientists at a lab are all seeking the same truths, trying to achieve the same goals.

It might not be nine to five, but it was hard work. Back in his hotel room, Cox would avoid reading about science or physics or his brain would begin whirring again. Rather, he would read books such as *God Is Not Great* by Christopher Hitchens. Others were beginning to recognise his academic talents, too. In October 2005, he became a Royal Society University Research Fellow. The oldest scientific academy in continuous existence and charged with championing and developing the pursuit of science in the UK and around the world, the University Research Fellow scheme is one of their flagship early career awards, given to elite scientists in their year group. Each year, there are 600 applicants and around 12 fellows are made, following close scrutiny of a five-year research proposal by a panel of experts. They also examine publication records and collect some background material on the candidate.

The award can be extended for three more years (as Cox did) and is considered an investment in the fellow himself rather than funding for a specific piece of research. Matching his university salary, with some subsistence costs on top, it is aimed at giving him the freedom to pursue different avenues during the fellowship. 'The idea is to bring the best scientists from our universities,' explains the Royal Society. 'We're down to the real cream of the crop.' Indeed, it was a prestigious pat on the back.

CERN was enthralling, but there was no doubt he was missing Gia and Moki. Though Cox tended to iChat with them on the computer before heading out for his evening meal, being away was difficult. It seemed as if it was time to take the next step in their relationship, though it appears that neither Brian nor Gia particularly cared for a big wedding. In fact, it was one of the smallest weddings ever. In 2004, they travelled to visit Milinovich's family in Duluth, Minnesota and while there were married in her mother's front room with a family friend who happened to be a judge officiating. 'It was kind of an afterthought, really,' he told the *Guardian*. 'We didn't make a big thing of it at all – we just wandered off and decided to get married. Because we didn't really want anyone there, to be honest.'

Cox's own parents were not very happy, having only been informed on the couple's return to the UK. 'I don't think they were entirely pleased,' he admitted, while attributing the decision as being partly down to his roots – 'I'm a northern man, I don't like any fuss.' He later joked that neither he nor his wife could remember exactly when it took place and that he needed to check at some point whether the ceremony had been legal. 'We felt quite strongly that it was about us and not anybody else,' he explained. 'It does seem quite eccentric in hindsight.' Since being awarded an OBE, people have suggested that he should exercise his right to marry in St Paul's Cathedral in London. 'I don't know whether that's apocryphal,' he said, 'but I've heard it so many times that it might be true. Maybe I should do it, just because I can. I won't, but it's an amusing thought, isn't it?'

While they didn't invite any guests, friends did get to see some pictorial evidence of the big day. 'I remember getting an email from Brian and Gia with photos of the wedding,' says the couple's former Network of the World colleague, Chiara Bellati. 'They had this very private, secret wedding and then they emailed a whole load of people announcing the happy news.'

The newly married couple began work on some science-based TV programme ideas and then Cox got a break: the BBC's *Horizon* was looking for contributors to a show they were doing called *Einstein's Unfinished Symphony*, a docudrama-style programme about the famous physicist's last project, which he hoped would unlock the mind of God. Narrated by actor Bernard Hill, the show mixes fictional scenes from Einstein's deathbed with commentary and talking heads. Cox was chosen to be the main interviewee. Not only did he explain the main scientific concepts throughout the programme, he was also asked to do some of the silent walking bits he would later emulate in his own series. At one point, he is filmed tossing a dice into the air in slow motion; elsewhere, he walks out of focus through an orchard. Interjected in these segments are abruptly angled interview shots as he lays out Einstein's ideas.

The show is a bit too tricksy in its attempts to sex up what is in essence a very straightforward documentary. Cox isn't as fluent as he would later become but he does a solid job and

Einstein's Unfinished Symphony received a 8.2 out of 10 user review rating on the Internet Movie Database. Though he had strived to break into the media properly for some time – and the BBC interest was a validation of that – Cox wasn't convinced about his on-screen ability. 'I never thought I could do it,' he told me in early 2010. 'When I first tried to do anything on TV, it was shit. I don't think many people are natural in front of cameras – I think in general you need practice. What the BBC have been brilliant at with me is thinking, he can probably do it eventually, let him have some practice. They've been very good and supportive.'

Einstein's Unfinished Symphony was broadcast in January 2005 and he quickly followed it up by participating in another BBC documentary called *Stardate: Comet Impact*, which was shown in the July. Suddenly, the Cox household had two television personalities. Milinovich had also been presenting for the BBC, on their World channel, with a show called *Click Online*. She had also teamed up in 2004 with co-presenter Ed Sanders for Channel 4's *Demolition Day*, an engineering reality show charging two teams with building indestructible edifices, which were then put at the mercy of their opponents, who attempted to smash them. Writing together seemed like a natural thing to do and they had done so before in their early television days at Network of the World. Now, they began to hatch up some interesting ideas with a view to talking to production companies.

Meanwhile, regular TV viewers will know that once a person appears on one show, inevitably they will show up again elsewhere, partly because producers are looking for a safe pair of hands but also because it is easier to hire someone who has already been on another show rather than look for fresh talent. Still, the brass at ITV was impressed by what they saw on the BBC and asked Cox to come in as a part-time contributor on *This Morning* to talk about any mainstream science issues that might crop up. He first appeared in March 2006 and went on to feature in another three episodes, alongside celebs such as Ant and Dec, as well as married tennis players Steffi Graf and Andre Agassi. Generally, his performances went down well, but there were some who were not so keen. One of his slots saw him talking about microwave devices and the possible adverse health effects. He discussed mobile phones and microwave ovens and how there was no particular evidence to suggest they caused damage to humans, as well as carrying out a small experiment over a short distance with microwaves. In addition, he talked about gadgets that purport to protect us from harmful microwave radiation, though in his capacity as a scientist, he didn't really seem to think much of them. In fact, he argued, the only way to truly protect oneself from microwaves would be to live in a metal box.

'Microwave ovens are obviously built to stop microwaves getting out,' he said. 'A metal box is the only way I know, as a scientist, of actually stopping that kind of radiation.' The creator of website www.nomasts.org took exception to the way Cox had presented the evidence, writing: 'Dr. Cox was unbelievable and grossly lacking in real information – and completely dismissive of any adverse health effects from these microwave emitting devices. On the subject of protection from microwave radiation, Dr. Cox just mentioned gimmicky items sold in shops.' Building up a head of steam, the piece continued: 'We challenge Dr. Cox to look into the evidence and studies carried out by Independent (sic) scientists – there is an ever-increasing amount of such studies. (We even sent him the details of some studies to start looking at.) All in all, an extremely poor presentation.'

Cox replied to the site, though it's difficult to tell quite how his response should be read, especially given his attitude to those working outside the scientific consensus. 'Thanks for your mail,' he wrote. 'I am relieved to have received this email, because I thought I was overly conciliatory, as a few of my colleagues suggested after watched the program (sic). My fear was that I was not harsh enough. Sitting inside a microwave oven would be an effective shielding technique for EM radiation in 1cm wavelength range, as we demonstrated. Cheers, Brian.' The media newbie had just received his first bad review.

Undeterred, Cox subsequently appeared on *BBC Breakfast* in May. Then, when Granada Television decided to make a daytime lifestyle show, his name was one that came up. Hosted by Fern Britton and filmed in Wiltshire, ITV's *Looking Good, Feeling Great* ran for 15 episodes during the summer of 2006. It featured Cox as the resident science guru, alongside life coach Pete Cohen and fitness trainer (and former actress) Julie Dawn Cole, who had also appeared with Cox on *This Morning*.

'It was about debunking some of the myths about the things you do to make yourself feel better,' explains Cole. 'Brian was the science part of it.' The programme-makers would come up with, for example, an old wives' tale that supposedly did something for your health and Cox would explain the method behind it in scientific terms. 'We'd look at fitness holistically,' says Cole, 'holistically and scientifically. He'd say the reason you feel better when you eat this is because there's a chemical in it that does such-and-such. That was how it worked.' And she appreciated Cox's input. 'I don't think you can separate science from [wellbeing],' she says. 'You have to look at the whole picture – that's really what we were trying to do.' Cole recalls a neophyte television presenter. 'He hadn't really done very much,' she adds. 'He was genuinely a really nice guy. It was a very happy show and he explained science in a way that you makes you think, I almost understand this. Only fleetingly! But he's passionate about his subject and that's what he brings to it.'

It was a view to be reiterated four years later when Cox's *Wonders* series were broadcast. Did Cole see a future star? 'I don't know,' she concedes. 'It's always about being in the right place at the right time but he's got a gift for making it sound very simple without pretence.' As each contributor waited to do their segment on-air with Fern Britton, Cole would chat with Cox in the Green Room. 'He's a very nice guy, very approachable, very unpretentious,' she says. 'And that's what he brings to science. That's a great gift. He didn't need [presenting advice].'

Though Gia was pleased and excited by her husband's new direction, she also began to sense the seeds of what would in 2010 lead her to pen an article for the *Guardian* about what she dubbed 'Invisible Wife Syndrome' (being married to a famous person – and being ignored because of it). It was particularly annoying in 2006 because the couple had some interesting programme ideas and both had a solid media presence. Unfortunately, that didn't seem to matter to one particular television executive. 'Brian and I went to pitch some ideas to a producer at a well-known production company,' wrote Milinovich. 'I'd had a science-technology series broadcast on Channel 4 several months earlier and Brian's appearances as the science expert on *This Morning* were going very well. Our agent called us the sci-tech version of Richard [Madeley] and Judy [Finnigan]. From the start, the producer's attention was on Brian. Every time I spoke, he'd look at me as though I was interrupting their conversation. At one point, I came out with what I thought was an excellent idea. The producer again turned towards me, said nothing, then slowly turned back to Brian. About a minute later, Brian repeated my idea almost word for word and the producer told him it was brilliant. As we left the building, I angrily told Brian how awful the whole experience was for me. Of course, he hadn't noticed a thing. As far as he was concerned, it was a very successful meeting with a very interesting and interested man.'

Milinovich argued she felt like Yoko Ono and the Beatles, as if she was breaking something up, even though the whole point of the meeting was to pitch ideas together. It was the beginning of the end for presenting, as far as she was concerned. After a few more meetings, she decided to concentrate less on TV and instead focus on her new media skills, producing and writing for websites, as well as working as a new media advisor and expert. 'Though I've accepted that Brian and I will probably never make any of the programme ideas we wrote when we first started working together,' she wrote, 'I'm happier not being the Yoko in our partnership.'

CHAPTER 7

GOING TO HOLLYWOOD

Many of his fans think Cox has movie star looks, so it's no surprise that Hollywood eventually came calling. It wasn't, however, as a leading man: director Danny Boyle was looking to follow his 2004 family comedy *Millions* with something a little meatier. Together with Alex Garland and producer Andrew Macdonald, with whom Boyle had collaborated on *The Beach*, he began developing an epic science fiction film called *Sunshine*. The project had started eight months before in Garland's mind. 'I've always had a desire to explore this idea of a man travelling into deep space and what he discovers there, as well as what he finds in his own subconscious,' he explains. 'I had been looking for a storyline to hang this idea on when I read an article projecting the future of mankind from a physics-based perspective. It contained theories on when the sun would die and what would actually happen when it eventually did. What I found interesting about that was that it was easy to speculate about the potential end of mankind, billions of years from now – but what if it was a certainty within our lifetime? I was intrigued by the idea that it could get to a point where the entire planet's survival might rest on the shoulders of one man and by the question of what that would do to his head. That became the trigger point for the story.'

Garland worked on a first draft, then met Boyle in a London pub to see whether he would be interested in signing on. The auteur was concerned about doing a schlocky blockbuster, but after listening to Garland's pitch, he realised that despite the need for a large budget (ultimately around $50 million), both were thinking of something more psychological. 'Travelling to the sun is great concept, visually but also very interesting, psychologically,' says Boyle. 'There is the question about what happens to your mind when you meet the creator of all things in the universe, which for some people is a spiritual, religious idea and for other people is a purely scientific idea. We are all made up of particles of exploded star, so what would it be like to get close to the sun, the star from which all the life in our Solar System comes from? I thought it would be a huge mental challenge to try and capture that.'

Essential for the filmmakers was to ensure the science in the work was as sound as possible. They met with personnel at NASA and chatted about the movie's concepts with astronauts and others such as Richard Seymour, a futurist designer. 'He's a blue skies thinker for people like Ford and Phillips,' says Boyle. 'He gave us an image of the future.' While it was important to create a design for the film that mixed the aesthetically pleasing with the realistic, Boyle and his team needed someone to advise on the specific elements of science within the script. Then in 2005, the director and his producer happened to be watching a BBC *Horizon* documentary called *Einstein's Unfinished Symphony* and immediately realised they had their man. 'They knew that one of the main characters in the film – Capa the physicist – was a young guy, about 30 years old,' said Cox on the film's DVD commentary. 'They knew he's got to be the best physicist in the world. So, the best physicist in the world being 30 years old bothered them because their impression of physicists is someone who looks like Einstein, some old guy with crazy hair and bad teeth. They saw me on the documentary and I don't look old.'

Macdonald and Boyle contacted Cox to ask if he would be interested in participating. 'It was one of the strange things that happens to you, where you get an email from Danny Boyle,' Cox told Radio 4. 'But actually it wasn't quite that simple because they sent it first to my PhD supervisor by accident. And through some correspondence they'd said to him, "We think you'd be an excellent role model, there's going to be a young actor playing the physicist and we think you're ideal for it because you're a great role model for young scientists." At that point he realised they were after *me*! It was one of those things where we both thought it was a joke at one point, because you don't expect a director like Danny Boyle to get in touch with you and say "Would you like to work on my film?" It sounds like someone's trying to wind you up.'

For Cox, the idea presented a unique challenge because it would mean balancing his credibility as a real scientist with

Hollywood's need for spectacular fiction. He was an unabashed *Doctor Who* fan and had also grown up passionate about *Star Wars*. 'I just grew up in that atmosphere,' he explained, 'so by the time *Star Wars* came along in 1977, I wanted to see it. I went to see that and was obsessed. I'd watched *Star Trek* all the way. When *Alien* came out in 1979, I was 11 and I saw it. Brilliant! I've always been like that and the only thing I can think of is just my dad being so interested in *Apollo* moon landings and that somehow filtered through.'

As a result of his childhood obsessions, he had a specific idea of how sci-fi needed to be treated. 'I am completely un-pedantic about science fiction,' he has said on the subject of *Who*. 'I think it's about ideas and I have no issue at all with it. It drives me mad, actually, when people go "Huh! That can't happen! That dalek just flew!" Science fiction comes from the same source as scientific thought, which is the desire to explore, think and dream about the universe and what's out there. Obviously, it's the same and when I was growing up, I couldn't really tell the difference. It feels like part of the same quest to me.'

Nevertheless, he didn't want *Sunshine* to appear foolish but the idea of flying into uncharted space fascinated him and if he wasn't going to do so in real life, maybe celluloid would be a reasonable substitute. Luckily, he received a reassurance from Boyle. 'Danny said to me really early on that he wasn't making a documentary,' said Cox at the time. 'But he wanted to make a film realistic enough that he didn't want to jar anybody, he didn't want to break the spell. You do really silly things – characters particularly do really stupid things that people recognise as being totally unscientific. All this techno babble that goes on in *Star Trek*, like tachyon fields and all that. I think it happens in *Event Horizon* and people turn off with all that bullshit. So we had to make sure none of that happened, because we might not have recognised if Alex happened to have written a load of crap down somewhere. [Luckily] Alex Garland is a fan of science, as well as a science fiction fan. There were a few edges we ironed out, but basically it was the backstory rather than the plot that my expertise was needed for.'

The movie also offered Cox a chance to deal with scientific matters that had interested him for some time, as well as grappling with some heady concepts. Namely, if the sun is going to die, why should we do anything about it? Surely it is nature taking its course. 'We know fairly accurately that the universe is 13.7 billion years old. The sun is four-and-a-half billion,' he says. 'When the universe began, there was only hydrogen and helium in the universe, just the two simplest elements. Now I can look at my hand, and it's red because there's iron in there, and carbon and oxygen. They came from somewhere, they came from stars. The only place you can make those things is in the centre of a star – that's what stars do, they stick things together; that's how they work. So, a star has got to do that and all that stuff is inside the star but when it runs out of fuel, it dies. And eventually it swells up and collapses and explodes. And when it explodes all that stuff gets out and goes out into the universe, re-collapses eventually under the force of gravity, these dust clouds, into new stars. They live, and they burn things, and they die. So, the stuff inside the sun and inside the earth has probably been through that cycle twice, so it's the third time for that stuff. The reason that stuff is here, and we're here, is because two generations of stars lived and died so it's important that they die.'

In other words, one might argue, what's happening now is merely the gestation period for the next thing that comes along. 'It is, without that you wouldn't have any heavy elements,' he explains. 'And by heavy, I mean anything other than hydrogen and helium, which would be a very boring universe. [The villainous character] Pinbacker says this, he says we're all stars and came from stardust and we'll all go back to stardust. Why are you worried, basically? He just thinks nature should take its course and he's right in a way.'

The film's plot was pretty simple. It's 2057 and the sun has started to die. The earth is trapped in solar winter and a mission to re-ignite the sun using a nuclear weapon appears to have failed because the ship has fallen off the radar. A second mission is now underway on a spacecraft known as the *Icarus II*. Populated by eight of the best astronauts and scientists on the planet, they are nearing their destination when they hear a distress call from the first ship. Though the *Icarus I* appears to be deserted, the crew soon realises they have unleashed something unpleasant and it's a race against time to reach the sun and detonate the Manhattan-sized bomb they've been carrying in order to save mankind. Pivotal to this effort is physicist Robert Capa, the only person capable of detonating their unique payload, while his colleagues include biologist Corazon and psychologist Searle, among others.

A slew of famous actors were hired to fill out the cast, including *Batman Begins'* Cillian Murphy as Capa, former Bond girl Michelle Yeoh (Corazon) and *Troy's* Rose Byrne as pilot Cassie. Though Cox was to work with the whole cast, he would pay specific attention to Murphy, whose character is described as an outsider.

'He's a scientist who is into a level of physics that is way beyond normal comprehension and that does something to his mind in a way,' says the actor. 'He doesn't have great people skills, though, which keeps him removed from the rest of the crew.' Added Cox: 'One of things I really like about Cillian's performance is you feel he's not a career astronaut, which he isn't. He will have spent most of his time doing what I do. Now he's been thrust into this position, 16 months out, 60 million miles from home, and the responsibility of saving the human race has been put on his shoulders.'

Ironically, Boyle's desire to find a young scientific advisor was somewhat reflected on-screen. 'For those who think he's a bit good-looking for a physicist,' says the director, 'the uncanny thing is that he looks remarkably like our science advisor Brian Cox, which was not intentional.' Cox himself enjoyed the comparison, telling one interviewer that if anyone could play him in the movie of his life, it would be Cillian Murphy. 'Because he did a good job last time!' he joked. The handsome Irish star is not the only person suggested by Cox – Johnny Depp was another suggestion. 'But not in any film apart from *Charlie and the Chocolate Factory*,' he laughs.

Lookalike or not, it was the characters of Capa and Corazon that really drew Cox in. 'The reason I was really committed to it when I read the script was the portrayal of scientists in it,' he says, 'particularly Capa, but also Michelle's character. The scientists are real, they don't say anything stupid and they behave like scientists. It's wonderful, actually, from Alex [Garland] because he didn't know me or any other scientists at the time and yet he managed to write these realistic scientists.' CERN backed the film, meaning that Cox could suspend his activities there to work on the project. 'The reason they like it is that everyone understands that they weren't out to make a documentary but millions of people were going to see it,' he explains. 'So if a generation of people grow up and you say "physicist" and they say "Cillian Murphy", you say "biologist" and they say "Michelle Yeoh", that's brilliant. [What's great is] the fact the film had a hero who's a physicist and really importantly, it's nature that causes the problem. It's not some mad scientist or our knowledge which causes the problem, it's just nature. The universe is violent and inhospitable, it's threatening and it will get us one way or another.'

So, Cox set to work and Gia managed to snag a job on the movie, too: as a website designer. 'There was so much research done for this film,' says actor Chris Evans, who plays the macho officer Mace. 'Everyone involved really got our hands dirty to understand what these characters are going through and what the movie is about.' First off, he had to come up with a reason as to why the sun might be dying in the first place. General scientific theory suggests the sun has enough energy to last for another 5 billion years or so. So why was it dying in the 21st century? Cox went away and hatched a plan. He read an academic paper suggesting there were exotic objects known as supersymmetric particles drifting around the universe that could be as old as the Big Bang. For the purposes of sunshine, he extrapolated that a huge collection of these particles may have drifted back into the sun (which is, after all, a star). Like cancer, they would eat away at the star, destroying it from within. It would be impossible to re-ignite the sun but Cox's theory was that these particles could be disrupted by a big enough bomb, so removing the cancer and setting the sun's fusion reactions back on track. As he himself said: 'This might be far-fetched, but it is allowed by certain theories of a sub-atomic world.'

Funnily enough, on the Sunshine DVD commentary, he makes a £10 bet with the viewer that by 2017, super-symmetrical particles will have been discovered at CERN. As of the end of 2011, results from the Large Hadron Collider actually suggest they don't exist. Professor Jordan Nash, who was working on one of the LHC experiments, told *BBC News*: 'The fact that we haven't seen any evidence of it tells us that either our understanding of it is incomplete, or it's a little different to what we thought – or maybe it doesn't exist at all.'

And the sun's problems were not the only issue he examined. The spacesuits worn by the astronauts in the film are made of gold, rather than the usual white. Although they are visually stunning, Cox did an experiment to see how close one could get to the sun with gold. He told Boyle and Garland that the bomb (originally said to have the mass of the moon) should be scaled down to Manhattan because the rockets required to power the initial idea would be practically impossible to build. In addition, he had several discussions with the screenwriter about the psychology of long-term spaceflight and more specifically, those who would do anything to prolong the human race and those who believe life is innately meaningless in the sense that the universe is forever expanding. Both are key concepts of the movie and Cox's sanguine outlook on the latter issue in particular perturbed his movie colleagues.

'In that universe, no life can exist forever, absolutely none,' says Cox. 'No legacy can be left, in principle, forever. That really bothered [Alex]. I've had loads of conversations with him about it and I smile when I say it because I don't care. It doesn't bother me – it's a long time in the future. We live in this immense universe and when you know that, that sense of perspective can do two things to you: it can either make you in awe of it and feel nature's an amazing thing, and make you feel like you want to look at it and think about it and investigate it. Or you can kind of go the other way, and just shrink and think it's too much and we're insignificant.' This must be part of the reason why Cox was drawn to the film: it debates the issue of religion, man versus nature and science in subtle ways that appealed to the avowed atheist. In the plot, there is Capa, who does everything in his power to save what he perceives to be a valuable Solar System, an important civilisation. Then there's the villain of the piece (no spoilers here), someone who believes mankind is simply a transient piece of the puzzle that is the ever-expanding universe and attempts to foil the mission.

'The physicist reacts to it the way I would,' says Cox. 'Then there's the fundamentalist, who thinks it's all too much, we're completely pointless and we should all go away. To me, he's a religious fundamentalist. I think what you have to recognise is in this "meaningless" universe, there're still sparks of meaning in it and the sparks of meaning are people. The incredible thing about the universe is that beings like us evolved and even though we're here for a small amount of time, we're still important enough for us to try and save.' He kept returning to the subject of what space travel over long periods would do to the human mind. 'These astronauts on *Icarus II* have been there for 16 months before the film begins, cooped up inside this small space together,' he explained. 'There's this very famous quote from one of the Russian cosmonauts that if you lock two or three men up in a container for months on end without access to their loved ones, then you have all the conditions for murder. There's a beautiful picture taken by *Voyager 2*, which was one of the first spacecraft that went out to Saturn and Jupiter, Neptune and Uranus. There's a picture of the earth and the moon hanging in space, beautiful crescents. It just shows you how absolutely fragile we are. And when you read a lot of the writings of the *Apollo* astronauts, when you look back [on] the whole earth, that sense of perspective is very affecting.

'I like to think that these astronauts that have been looking at the earth receding away until it's just a speck in the sky for 16 months would [have] started to ask these profound questions which are dealt with [towards the end of] the film. One of the things that space does to you, or it certainly does to me – I wanted to be a physicist and an astronomer from a very young age, it gives you perspective.'

He also had input on features such as Corazon's Oxygen Garden, which in the movie is the source of the ship's air supply, using his scientific knowledge in a more theoretical arena. 'The Oxygen Garden was another piece of accuracy, I think, on the ship,' he said. 'It's absolutely clear that one of the problems in a three-year mission is oxygen and plants are a beautiful way of taking carbon dioxide and turning it into oxygen. So there was this wonderful Oxygen Garden on the ship and I think that's probably the way you'd do that if you're going on a manned mission to Mars. I'm sure there'd be plants on the ship and maybe they'd be the primary life support system.'

He also tackled one of the most debated inaccuracies in sci-fi movies – the existence of artificial gravity on board the spacecraft. Acknowledging the only way to truly achieve this would be to have a rotating ship (like the design Stanley Kubrick uses in *2001: A Space Odyssey*), he also suggests it's an acceptable flaw in a film and that Boyle adds a nod to it by having one part of the ship spinning. Some people didn't agree, such as Ajana Ahuja, who lambasted the scientific inaccuracy in *The Times*. Eagle-eyed critics also picked up on other 'errors' – among them, the moment when a character says the outside temperature is completely zero (-273°C), whereas space is actually 3° warmer. It annoyed Cox, who felt such viewers were on the wrong track. '

I don't mind geeks being geeks, I like it – I'm a geek myself,' he told Adam Rutherford on Radio 4. 'So it's interesting to see these debates on the Web about the science that was wrong. But if you try and judge the worth of a film by a pedantic reaction to a certain thing in the film, I think you really are missing the point.' He also suggested that in the movie, it's the biologist Corazon who has the temperature line and it's perfectly valid that she – not a physicist – would get it wrong. In fact, he suggested to Rutherford some things about space travel simply cannot be recreated for cinematic audiences. 'We discussed how space would look from a spacecraft and if you look at pictures from *Apollo*, there are no stars visible in the sky because it's light inside and dark outside. Danny tried that – not have stars and not to have sound from the spacecraft because that's another common gripe, but you find it looks entirely wrong, it doesn't work. [It] proves you can get the science right and provide a less realistic experience for the cinema-going audience – there's a cinematic shorthand.'

But while the filmmakers wanted Cox's input on some of the more generic elements of the story, perhaps the most important job he did for them was in coaching the actors in scientific equivalent of boot camp. To recreate the claustrophobia of the *Icarus II*, Boyle placed all his actors in tightly knit dormitories in east London, forcing them into close contact. 'In the film, we join the crew when they have been living together on a spaceship for 16 months,' explains Boyle. 'One of the key things was to get the cast to bond as quickly as possible and break down any barriers. The actors thought they'd be living in a big house together, so the single room, student-style accommodation was a bit of an unpleasant shock yet it was crucial.'

'There's a certain kind of chemistry you can't act,' says Cillian Murphy. 'It's just in the room, in the chemistry between people, that familiarity or irritability, or whatever it may be.' With the performers in close proximity, it was time for Cox to turn them into scientists, or at least make them appear savvy within that environment. Boyle asked his scientific advisor to give an initial lecture to the cast on general physics – about CERN, the sun and particle physics – so they were able to see how a scientist talked. When Cox had first met the director and screenwriter Garland, he had warned that they might have to put up with a few things. One was that he would try and tell

Boyle how to direct the film and he would also tell Garland how to write it. He explained it was a trait of scientists.

Rather than balk, ever the collaborator Boyle embraced it. 'Cillian told me one of the things Danny said to the cast was that they should listen to me when somebody said something that I thought was stupid,' says Cox on the film's DVD. 'I'd just say no really, really definitively. I think that's a trait of not only scientists but all academics and Cillian told me Danny told the rest of the cast to listen to me when someone said something stupid to me and listen to the dismissive nature of my response.' Cox certainly notices this in some of the cast's behaviour while delivering their lines, whether it's actor Troy Garity being dismissive of the other characters when they don't believe he's heard a distress call, or when Capa reacts to the news that the ship has been damaged because one of the crew has neglected to correctly alter the shield's co-ordinates.

Since he had been hired because of his similarity in age to the character of Capa – and because he was the ship's physicist – it was inevitable that Cox focused mainly on working with star Cillian Murphy. 'He's a very nice man, who put up with all my idiotic questions,' says the actor. Cox took Murphy to CERN, where he sat in on meetings. 'He said to me later one of the things he likes to do is pick up small things that will allow him to build a character, so he doesn't act like himself,' said Cox. Some of that included taking on specific characteristics of his mentor. While shooting a video diary scene in the film, Murphy can be seen pressing his hands together in front of his face, almost, ironically, as if he's praying. It's something Cox's friends tell him he does.

Some of the real-life scientist's work even made it into the movie: on the walls of Capa's bunk. The set designers wanted some papers with equations written on them to pin up in the character's sleeping quarters, work he could have already done or was doing. What the audience sees is actually a bunch of research papers written about what might happen when the Large Hadron Collider is turned on and since published in academic journals. Murphy was also intrigued by the brutality with which scientists treat each other in meetings when it comes to their work. He brings that into the movie at several moments, startling Cox, who recognises it as one of his least agreeable traits. This sits alongside his scientist's comfort when it comes to what is outside his knowledge. 'I'm very comfortable with saying "I don't know",' he says. 'I'm comfortable with just not knowing and keep prodding away. I talked to Cillian a lot about this. There's a certainty in science and the certainty in the happy existence of the things I know, and the things I don't know. I'm happy and smiling, and I'll keep chipping away at these things.'

He also worked hard with Murphy on some of the moral conundrums thrown up by the story. Capa has to react to several scenarios in a fairly cruel way, but Cox was keen to ensure the filmmakers knew this would be the physicist's way. 'There's a great scene when they're talking about killing [a character] because they need more oxygen,' remembers Cox. 'They go round the table and it gets to Cillian and he really quickly says "What are you asking me to do, weigh the life of one against a whole civilisation? Kill him." It's absolutely right, morally and logically correct. But I was talking to Danny and he said to me "You know that's what Stalin did in a way? He just said, I kill two million people but ten million people are better off." Danny thinks you should deal with the person in front of you, don't try weighing this against this then you go on your own slippery slope. That's in the film, it's nice.'

When it hit cinemas in April 2007, the movie met with mixed results. The Internet Movie Database says it made just over $24.5 million at the worldwide box office and it retains a 75 per cent score on Rotten Tomatoes, a collation of various reviews. Philip French in the *Observer* wrote: '*Sunshine* is remarkable for the technical virtuosity with which it creates life on a space vehicle and the cosmos around it.' Stephanie Zacharek praised Cillian Murphy's performance in particular on Salon.com: 'The picture would be nothing, an incomplete Venn diagram, without Murphy. [He] pulls off the near-impossible task of making saving earth look like something you just do without thinking.' Many critics praised Boyle's ambition and lauded the way he focused on the psychology of space travel. Others lambasted the last third of the movie when the baddie begins to wreaks havoc on the crew, claiming it made an otherwise thoughtful work into something more straightforwardly genre. Some picked up on the filmmakers' dedication to 'good' science. 'It belongs to that select group of science-fiction films that care more about the science than the fiction,' argued Brandon Fibbs in the *Colorado Springs Gazette*. Meanwhile on Digital Spy, Ben Rawson-Jones wrote: '*Sunshine* is a fantastically enjoyable film that works our minds, delights our senses and shows that futuristic science fiction can be serious drama rather than mere popcorn fodder.'

For his part, Cox thoroughly enjoyed the experience. 'I'd recommend it, actually,' he said. 'If you ever get called up by Danny Boyle and he says, "Do you want to work on my film?", I would recommend it!' And he saw a lot of his chosen career in the process of making a movie. 'One of things I've taken away from this experience of working on a film – it's the first one I've worked on – is the attention to detail,' he recalled. 'Obviously I knew these films took many years to put together but the final film is only one hour forty and every bit's been thought about and discussed. I was involved in a lot of discussion of various scenes.'

The experience also provided him with a rare though much appreciated chance to reflect on the path he had taken into science. Speaking to Radio 4, he said: '[The filmmakers] want you to express to them what it is about science that you love and you fear. Really, to understand what you perceive as the beauty of the science; what motivated you to become a scientist as a kid, because the actor wants that in their mind. Sometimes you forget that. If you're a professional scientist, or indeed a professional in many areas, when you become focused on the minutiae of your job you forget the bigger picture and you forget what motivated you to do it in the first place. And I've always thought, certainly since *Sunshine*, I've realised doing science is an emotional reaction to nature. Because it was once when you were the kid who looked up at the stars and thought the sky was beautiful and fascinating, and wanted to be an astronomer. That's an emotional reaction. So, to be reminded of that constantly because someone is trying to extract that out of you in order to put it on-screen is a very refreshing experience, actually.'

Cox told friends he felt as if he had undergone free psychoanalysis as a result of participating in the film. He revelled in spending time on the set at 3 Mills Studios, near Bromley-by-Bow in London, watching in awe as actor Hiroyuki Sanada performed a particularly emotional scene against a green screen. And he was amused to see Mark Strong, playing the heavily burned, malevolent character Pinbacker, during his downtime. 'We'd see Mark Strong in his outfit, reading the *Guardian*,' he remembers. 'He was obviously thinking of it, getting annoyed, but he was also making salad and running around and delivering his performance.' He also enjoyed watching the finished shots, where Capa has to do something action-y. It was where the child in him triumphed over the mature adult, such as when Capa gets stuck in an airlock as the clock ticks away. 'Capa as a physicist has been given this challenge, he's been given this problem, which is one of the things we all like as scientists,' said Cox. 'He's locked in the airlock – he's got a few things in there. He's got a spacesuit and luckily, he's got a blowtorch. He's got to find some way of getting out of the airlock.'

Despite reading it in the script, the finale involving Cillian Murphy coming face-to-face with his destiny ended up being one of the most emotional moments for Cox. Together with Boyle and Garland, he had discussed the moment when Capa reaches out his hand to touch what appears to be the surface of the sun but nothing had prepared him for the finished special effect and the trio argued about what the image meant. The director preferred to see it as meeting God. As a non-believer, Cox was never going to agree, but instead thought: 'He's been brought face-to-face with the beauty of nature, which is why he's a physicist. Perhaps for the first time he's really understood what it was that made him study nature all his life.' He saw the film with a number of scientific colleagues and they all admitted they found the final moments extremely powerful. It was helped, in his opinion, by the music from Manchester band Underworld.

Boyle himself reflected on what he was trying to say afterwards and indicates his discussions with Cox were an important influence, especially their debates about science versus something bigger, as well as the potential consequences of CERN. 'One of the themes for me is how arrogant science is. You talk with Brian Cox enough and you get this slight sense that they can do anything. And with [the Large Hadron Collider], they clearly think they can find this particle that existed after the Big Bang. He said there is a less than 10 per cent chance that it could create a black hole and you think, wouldn't that mean we're all dead? And he said you wouldn't know anything about it, nobody will know anything about it – the whole galaxy will collapse into this black hole if it happens. He said it's probably not going to happen and anyway when they exploded the first atom bomb, they told Congress there was a small chance they could set the world on fire – the whole planet – and they decided to go ahead anyway. So you have to be vainglorious in that way.'

Cox wasn't so interested in the concepts of scientific hubris. Rather, the movie was about reconnecting with his love for nature and its awesome power. He was also keen to use *Sunshine* as a cog in one of his familiar treatises: we have to get out there and explore. What moved him was: 'Those issues, the fact that nature is violent and it's not necessarily safe on this planet and the only chance we've got of doing anything about that is learning about the universe. It seems obvious, but I can't think of another film that actually says that. And it's true, it's correct and that's why I love the film.' The collaboration with Boyle and co. was so successful that there were promises of working together again. 'Danny said that he'd bring me back on board if he ever made another science-fiction film,' Cox told Shortlist. 'But he's since told me that he never will, so there you go.'

Sunshine was the first and biggest cinematic experience Cox has been a part of so far, but it's not the only one. It's worth noting that he received a credit of thanks on *Departure*, a short made by a group of students from the Arts University College at Bournemouth as their 2011 graduation film. Telling the story of two astronauts (James Lance and Camilla Rutherford) on a faraway spacecraft who have to make some tough decisions when their ship springs a leak, it echoes some of the themes of *Sunshine* but also takes its cue from other meditative sci-fi movies such as *Moon* or *Silent Running*.

'One of our lecturers had worked with [Cox] before and she recommended we get in contact with him,' says Ali Paterson, who produced *Departure* through his Inopean Films shingle, as well as contributing to the story as a writer and acting as art director. They phoned Cox's agent to be told he was busy, but to phone back a couple of months later and it would be possible for the director Duncan Christie to have a chat. 'Essentially, we were looking for a [scientific advisor],' says Paterson. 'I believe

Duncan Christie spoke directly to him and about the technical aspects of the film.' The agent also put them in contact with the National Space Centre in Leicester (the crew were told to mention Cox's name and they would get in for free). And so the production designers and those who built the sparse but effective sets travelled up to Leicester and Cox was as good as his word. 'They all had a good look round,' says Paterson. 'Brian got a thanks because we got that from them. We also spoke to Colin Pillinger from Mars Rover.'

The quietly haunting and well-acted short looks especially impressive for its student background and has proved to be Cox's second at least critical hit. Explains Paterson: 'It's just got into the Berlin Film Festival, so I'm pretty chuffed.'

CHAPTER 8

THE BBC COMES KNOCKING...

Back at CERN, the countdown had begun to switch on at the Large Hadron Collider. In May 2007, Cox participated in another BBC *Horizon* show, *The Six Billion Dollar Experiment*, in which he faced the camera against a black background and talked about the switch-on date. When the programme was made, it was scheduled to be 26 November of that year, but it was of course put back. During this time, the price of the project was often being mentioned and the cost to the taxpayer, even though the scientists working there constantly said this was nothing compared to what they would be achieving.

Money was an easy target for the UK press, whose front pages were filled with stories of a financial crisis and recession. Why, some said, should the British public be spending money on something that *might* discover a new particle? Cox re-iterated the technological advances CERN had brought to the world, such as the internet. 'Also, medical imaging,' he said. 'Pretty much all of the medical imaging technology that we use today came from particle physics. It's a spin-off of trying to understand how the world works. Again. Virtually everything is, but that's a direct one – PET scanners, or positron-emission tomography. Positron is anti-matter. You need to understand anti-matter to have a PET scanner.' But he was firm on the fact that in his eyes, the project was incredible value for money. 'Its budget,' he said, 'as of which it was built and as of which it operates, is the same as my university. It's the same as the budget of the University of Manchester, but 85 countries pay for it so it's like one medium-sized European university. You also only need one in the world, fortunately. It's either expensive or cheap, depending on which way you look at it. So whether or not that's expensive is a matter of perspective, isn't it? I think it's pretty cheap.'

To counter-act any negative publicity, CERN launched a PR offensive and Cox was brought in to help. Beginning in April 2007, he hosted a series of podcasts, explaining that he would be inviting a series of famous people to come to CERN and experience what it was like there. 'We're going to get a sense through their eyes of what it means to look back in time to the origins of the universe,' he said. He received a £10,000 grant from the Science and Facilities Training Council (STFC) to do so, with the remit to produce the podcast and an accompanying blog, which would include a section about the particle of the month. His first guest was the actor John Barrowman, star of *Doctor Who* spin-off *Torchwood*, who Cox described as, 'one of the most famous people, I suppose, in science fiction.'

Chatting in the canteen and then on a tour round the facilities, Cox explained the concept of the multiverse to the wide-eyed star, who joked about the presenter's 'big ring', adding: 'It's nice to be able to see where all of these questions that we have hopefully one day will be answered.' It was clear that Cox was already becoming the public face of the LHC, especially if they were going to host British 'celebs' on the podcast. Standing in the LHC tunnel, Barrowman marvelled at its size, suggesting a scene where he ran the length of it. 'We could call it "The Collision",' he said, 'waiting for me to collide with somebody running the opposite direction. We could simulate what is happening down here.' Cox laughed, replying: 'It would be an extremely boring *Torchwood* episode!'

The pair joked about what kind of quark Barrowman would be and Cox was asked to sign a picture from the cameras on ATLAS ('It looks like some kind of jet engine,' said the actor), so that Barrowman could put up a framed picture of some atoms smashing together in his office. The positive publicity continued to the end of the programme. 'Having seen it today, I'm totally amazed at the minds of the people and the creativity that goes into the creation of finding out where everything was created,' said a rather muddled Barrowman. 'You might just be the answer to world peace.'

The raft of famous people for the remaining 11 episodes never really materialised, though and instead Cox chatted to characters such as MP Ed Vaizey and comedian Kevin Eldon. Television presenters Ant McPartlin and Declan Donnelly expressed an interest in visiting, something Cox had not arranged at the time of writing. He did manage to get someone to visit which caused a small flurry in the Web-o-sphere – notoriously taciturn satirist Chris Morris. The writer and director behind the film *Four Lions* and shows such as *The Day Today* is a friend of Cox and a huge science fan. Though Cox preferred to talk about politics when they met, he always felt Morris steered the conversation towards CERN. 'He doesn't usually do things like that, but he was really fascinated by what we were doing there,' said Cox. 'So I said, "You should come out and see it for yourself." He's fanatically interested in everything.'

Enjoying his tour around the LHC, Morris managed to stump his friend when he said Cox had told him the LHC could destroy the universe, a charge he denied suggesting he merely wanted to scare his friend into putting more chilli into the meal he was preparing for him at the time. One thing CERN certainly didn't do was pursue a rather deadly and anti-Swiss strategy for getting young people to see the complex – a far-fetched gag, which Cox explained in a comedic interview on the website www.neonbubble.com. 'I realised that kids simply weren't getting to see inside CERN in Geneva owing to the general Swiss fear of small people,' he said. 'Well, I like kids – I used to be one – and so I devised a competition where we would place special tickets inside special bars of special chocolate and allow the winners to tour. It was a great success. All the children died in horrific ways – high doses of X-rays, falling in the particle streams, accelerating to near the speed of light, that sort of thing – but the small print covered us. The Swiss were quietly pleased. They don't like small people. It's those clocks where the small people come out, you see. There's a collective terror in Switzerland.'

Those who were part of the LHC were working non-stop and

unconcerned about conspiracy theories coming from the outside world, fuelled by the many coffee machines dotted around the laboratory. In November of the previous year, Cox's experiment ATLAS had made a huge leap forward, revving its barrel toroid magnet – the largest superconducting magnet ever built – up to its maximum current (21,000 amps). By June 2007, the team were lowering its two end magnets, each weighing 240 tonnes, into the tunnel. A month later, the new biometric system was being finalised, which meant Cox had to have his retinas scanned every time he went down into the LHC tunnel for security. That was important – people were beginning to talk about the project and with ATLAS alone costing £245 million just in materials, there was a lot to lose.

With almost 3,000 scientists from 38 countries represented too, no one could wait to get started on recreating the conditions less than one billionth of a second after the Big Bang in order to see what must have happened and how the universe as we know it was formed. Not only that, but physicists were itching to begin the search for the Higgs boson. In his trademark style, Cox described this on *The Six Billion Dollar Experiment*. 'The best theory we have for the origin of mass, or what makes stuff stuff, is called the Higgs mechanism,' he said. 'And the Higgs mechanism works by filling the universe with a thing, it's almost like treacle. And by the universe, I don't just mean the void between the stars and the planets – I mean the room in front of you. And some particles move through the Higgs field, and talk to the Higgs field and slow down, and they're the heavy particles so all the particles that make up your body are heavy because they're talking to the Higgs field.'

His fellow scientist Leon Lederman added to the description. 'The Higgs brings simplicity and beauty to a nature that looks too complicated,' he said. 'It makes nature simpler than we think it is. It introduces a kind of symmetry, a kind of beauty that gives us an understanding of one of the most puzzling features of the Standard Model.' Cox, however, was one of the scientists at CERN who believed that while the LHC was partly built in order to discover the Higgs boson, the fact that it might not be found would prove equally valuable and make the LHC just as valid.

'It can be argued that the most interesting discovery would be that we cannot find the Higgs – proving, practically, that it isn't there,' said his colleague, the Spanish physicist Alvaro de Rujula. 'That would mean that we really haven't understood something. That's a very good scene for science. Revolution sometimes comes from the fact that you hit a wall and you realise you truly haven't understood anything.' His views echoed those espoused by Cox, even during his tenure as *Sunshine*'s scientific advisor: that he doesn't mind being wrong if it means he has the tools and the next steps to try and find out what is correct.

While he waited for work on ATLAS and the LHC to be finished at CERN, Cox was busy furthering his television career. 'There was a period of getting celebrities to do science programmes,' he told an audience at the Edinburgh Television Festival, 'but now it's academics doing it. There's a conscious decision to turn academics into presenters and celebrities. It's the opposite of *The X Factor*.'

He was drafted in by his local BBC news magazine

programme *North West Tonight* as their science guru; radio presenter Tony Livesey later said this was Cox's big break, an over-exaggeration but it proved a useful, if brief practice ground. Fronting a series of segments dubbed 'Appliance of Science', he visited colleagues and places of interest in and around Manchester, examining the region's influence in the building of the world's first computer and exploring the importance of mathematics. As with later programmes, he demonstrated real-world examples of essentially abstract concepts, showing how Boeing used maths to help test the capacity of their airplanes to withstand lightning and how the fire service predict the ways fires will spread to help train their fire-fighters.

The beginning of 2008 also saw the first of three *Horizon* programmes broadcast that year. Titled *What On Earth Is Wrong With Gravity?*, it's the first time viewers were really able to witness the style for which Cox later became famous. Though previous television efforts had seen him either as a contributor or a talking head, finally the BBC were making good on what he thought they had first seen in him, back in 2005. The Beeb described the show thus and you can see how they were beginning to groom Cox to fill what they perceived to be a gap in their presenting roster – the cool scientist: 'Particle physicist and ex D:Ream keyboard player Dr Brian Cox wants to know why the universe is built the way it is. He believes the answers lie in the force of gravity. But Newton thought gravity was powered by God and even Einstein failed to completely solve it. Heading out with his film crew on a road trip across the USA, Brian fires lasers at the moon in Texas, goes mad in the desert in Arizona, encounters the bending of space and time at a maximum security military base, tries to detect ripples in our reality in the swamps of Louisiana and searches for hidden dimensions just outside Chicago.'

Speaking at the time, Cox explained why he wanted to tackle the subject. 'The biggest question in science is gravity at the moment,' he said, obviously ignoring the huge number of magnets getting ready to fire at his day job, about which he had waxed lyrical for some time. 'It's the force we thought we understood for the longest time, since 1680, but it still baffles us and stays separated from our understanding of everything else. We tried to work out a way of [conveying it] and ended up doing this road trip, because most of the places we wanted to go ended up being in the States.'

He was paired with writer/director Paul Olding for the project, a collaboration that would continue through *Wonders of the Universe* and beyond. 'We annoy each other with our questions,' said Olding. 'My physics questions to him and his biology questions to me (I am a biologist by training, you see – we compliment each other quite well).' Driving across the country, Cox sang along with Manchester band Inspiral Carpets to their single 'Saturn 5', while criticising the coffee for tasting like gravel. He had grown to love coffee, mainly thanks to his American wife and even blamed her for making him not able to function without it. Asked what luxury he would take, if stranded on Radio 4's *Desert Island Discs*, the answer was a coffee machine.

Filming wasn't all easy and his poor sense of direction did for them in Colorado. 'We got lost going to the Sat-Nav headquarters in Colorado Springs, using Sat Nav,' he remembered. 'It took us into a field instead of getting us to the military base.' Outtakes from the show reveal a man excited by the new challenge and still a little raw, not yet media-trained to within an inch of his life. He joked with the crew about looking young but insisted he did work in a physics lab and that he had the 'prowess' to present a serious TV programme. And he made fun of their accommodation, suggesting they had to stay in shoddy motels rather than decent hotels because of BBC budgetary constraints. He even put on a comedic working-class Manchester accent, observing that documentaries on the BBC were not about delivering information anymore, but about the audience experiencing a journey through the presenter's eyes.

It was also clear that Cox wasn't going to lose his physicist's knack of giving short shrift to those who asked silly questions. At a diner in Tucson, Arizona and obviously tired, he and Olding got into an argument about the exact nature of gravitational waves. When the director struggled to understand what Cox was trying to say – as the scientist simulated a wave using his napkin and asked if Olding was being deliberately obtuse – there was a brief, but fascinating insight into the way the programmes were made. As Cox grew more annoyed and the director tried to explain what he was asking, the suggestion was it was the directors as well as Cox who helped to make the shows more accessible to an audience, who would likely ask similar questions about a gravitational wave sitting on their sofas. That's not to say Cox was about to change the way he reacted to things he perceived as idiotic. 'I don't know whether it's because I'm from Oldham, but I believe in a straight-talking version of science,' he once said. 'There's nothing mystical about it. We are too delicate with people who talk crap sometimes.'

When Olding asked if they should mention that the moon landings have been alleged to be fake by some conspiracy theorists, Cox again grew tetchy, equating this to saying that America was never discovered. As Olding pushed him, Cox argued back that it would be inappropriate to talk about faked moon landings in a documentary about gravity and the matter came to a close. He admitted subsequently that he enjoyed getting angry, his friend and collaborator Robin Ince suggesting that he liked 'fighting with people and going, "look at those idiots."' Cox agreed, answering a question about his dream dinner guest with Deepak Chopra. 'I quite like controversial people – I like people I can argue with,' he said. 'I like being angry, so people who make me angry would be my ideal guests.'

Back then, he may not have been the superstar he has since become, but it's clear Cox knew even in those days what he would and would not do. Despite being scared about all the poisonous creepy-crawlies when he visited an experiment in Louisiana (and he seems genuinely frightened), Cox enjoyed the experience. It was a mostly a success too, garnering solid reviews if not entirely for the content, then for the presenter himself. 'Dr Brian Cox is an interesting presenter,' wrote a blogger on *The Medium is Not Enough*. 'He's personable, funny, knows what he's talking about, can explain it in simple terms and isn't a stereotypical science geek. He's also not afraid to scribble the occasional equation down, which is nice.'

Where the reviewer didn't get on board was with the very

issue which Cox had brought up during the filming – the desire of the channel making the show to concentrate on the personal journey. 'Thing is, about 60% of the documentary was all about Cox's journey around the U.S.,' they wrote, 'lots of shots of him in a truck; lots of shots of him on the subway; lots of shots of him standing looking up at telescopes. It's the kind of "people-centric" thing that appeals to the science-light science networks in the US, such as the Discovery Channel and Nova, and it's much in keeping with current trends in TV documentary-making, but it gets in the way of actual content.' The BBC, however, were not going to worry about such criticisms. After all, getting the audience to identity and empathise with their presenters was exactly what they wanted. And watching *What On Earth Is Wrong With Gravity?* it appeared that they might well have a star on their hands.

Though he had filmed two more *Horizons* to be shown later in the year, by mid-to-late summer Cox was consumed by the LHC. Because of his BBC profile – and Britishness – he had now become the designated spokesperson for the UK media on CERN and the switch-on date. During the open days at the beginning of April 2008, 76,000 people had visited and now people wanted action. In June, ATLAS was one of two experiments to close the LHC ring by installing beam pipes at their heart. Cox's experiment, his job, was now one of the biggest collaborations ever attempted in physics. The computer systems to record the information from what was essentially a giant digital camera were in place. Though ATLAS would only record fractions of the data it saw, this would still equate to the 27 CDs per minute. If all the data from ATLAS were recorded, it would fill 100,000 CDs per second. That's a transfer rate equivalent to 50 billion phone calls happening at the same time. Students, as Cox had been back in Hamburg, were working alongside the professional scientists in CERN and came from 172 institutes around the world.

Of the impending switch-on, CERN wrote: 'We will be re-writing our children's science textbooks, chapter by chapter. This experiment is the culmination of a lifetime of effort and the excitement is unlike anything we have experienced as scientists.' Cox was certainly feeling a change in atmosphere whenever he wandered into the complex's canteen for lunch. 'Particle accelerators are born very rarely and the LHC will be the lone explorer at the high-energy frontier when the smaller Tevatron collider in Chicago is decommissioned in the next few years,' he wrote in the *Guardian*. 'All our eggs will then be in one basket.'

There was a definite sense of the responsibility to get things right. And despite all the ingenuity and hard work that had gone into creating the enterprise, there was no way to escape the challenges they would face. When the machine was first turned on, Cox had told John Barrowman that they would be lucky to get two particles to bang together, let alone the millions they were eventually hoping for. 'A few weeks ago in the LHC control room, I asked one of the accelerator's designers what he would feel on switch-on day,' he said. '"It will be like threading a wet piece of cotton through the eye of a 27km-long needle," he said, "but we'll do it." He meant it, and I have no doubt that the LHC and its detectors will deliver the goods. I have no doubt that we will look back at the year the LHC switched on as the most exciting time for fundamental physics in a generation, or possibly in the long history of the subject. Everyone here knows it and this is what it feels like to be at CERN in 2008.'

Of course, the world might not have existed after the machine was turned on. At least that's what a lot of naysayers were talking about in the press and on the Web, arguing that the LHC would create a black hole which would swallow up the world, or that the collider was one of Nostradamus's predictions about the end of days made true. A journalist who interviewed Cox in 2008 recalls their conversation: 'I said to him jokily, "I've seen Event Horizon, I know if you create a black hole it creates a gateway to Hell." Very drily, he replied, "No one would be more surprised than me if that happened."' Not all the comments were so jocular. It was then that he uttered one of his most famous quotes, responding to the *Radio Times*' question about the dangers of the LHC in saying: 'Anyone who thinks that the LHC is dangerous is a twat.'

Papers dubbed him the 'Liam Gallagher' of physics. The press officer at CERN even phoned to say thank you. Cox himself wrote that he was glad to be able to challenge the image of scientists as tweed-wearing old men with elbow pads, 'carefully crafting their public pronouncements while strolling through hushed quadrangles beneath dreaming spires.' It got him headlines and when he gave a talk in Florida some time afterwards, he said that people almost saw it as his catchphrase. 'If you're lucky, you get one quote on your gravestone and that'll be mine,' he said.

In fact, he and his colleagues would have been pleased if the LHC had created small black holes, since that would suggest the existence of multiple universes, one of the very things ATLAS was set up to explore. He told Oreilly.com: 'Someone once said to me the trouble with conspiracy theories is because they've got no concept, no contact with reality anyway, then anything you say to them will be disregarded because the whole basis of their existence is that they ignore common sense. So you can't say anything to these guys except that come the day we turn the LHC on when nothing happens and the world doesn't end, I would like an apology from all of them for the shit that they've spoken for all these years. It won't come, though!'

Inevitably, his comments led to him being misquoted on several websites, who insinuated that he was anti anyone sceptical about new scientific endeavours. With hindsight, he offered a slight olive branch, but it was clear he was more interested in clearing up discrepancies than actually apologising for his tough words. Writing on the Scientificconcerns.com forum, he said: 'I'm quoted in [an] article posted here as being rather abusive to people who are worried about the LHC – I'd like to clarify! I certainly don't think that people who are worried about new scientific endeavours are "tw*ts"! Scepticism is a valuable and vital part of our society, and one which is perhaps sadly lacking in public debate. For the record, the concerns about LHC are certainly wrong from a scientific perspective – nature is rather more robust than we give her credit for, and nothing we can do at the low energies we can manage at LHC or anywhere else in the foreseeable future will affect us in any way. But I would always encourage a rational debate about future advances in science, and in that sense I support the goals of this forum.

What I would say is that it is not sensible to hold an opinion in the face of overwhelming evidence to the contrary. Whilst I understand that much of the language of particle physics is opaque, there does come a time when it is worth accepting the views of experts. The analogy I would give is the design of aircraft wings – I am happy to trust an expert in aerodynamics to get it right rather than offer my own opinion about what shape they should be. It's really the case that the particle physics community are sensible, rational human beings who go about their research because they believe that exploring the subatomic world is good for our civilization, not to mention interesting. It is also true that if anyone, including myself, had any doubt about the safety of what we are doing, we would stop immediately. I and all my colleagues consider our personal safety and the safety of our families to be FAR more important than the search for the Higgs particle – indeed, if the risk were even as high as 1 in a billion, or whatever people quote, then I would be campaigning with you to stop it. But honestly – the case advanced against the LHC is based on the rather loud pronouncements of a couple of people who really do not have the knowledge to make them. This "jtankers" chap who posts all over the place began one statement claiming that we collide particles together at twice the speed of light, and Otto Rossler, whilst clearly a distinguished biochemist, has based his argument on a pretty basic error in General Relativity. Now I am not criticizing these gentlemen for offering an opinion, but wisdom comes from noticing when one's opinion is disproved by evidence. This is the key to science. So, in summary, I support this forum as a place where sceptical voices can be raised, but scepticism must go hand in hand with rationality. When theories are shown to be false, the correct thing to do is to move on.'

To much fanfare and no Armageddon, the Large Hadron Collider was switched on for the first time on 10 September 2008. There was blanket coverage on Radio 4 and Google posted an image on their homepage that was seen by an estimated half a billion people. Gia tweeted her pride when her husband sat down on *Newsnight* with host Jeremy Paxman and the President of the British Association for the Advancement of Science, Sir David King, to argue the importance of the LHC. Paxman was glib about whether it was useful to spend money on a machine of this nature and Cox leapt passionately to its defence. More disappointingly for him, King also seemed ambivalent about the project, saying he was excited that it was happening, but also wondered whether money should be spent on more focused research.

It wasn't that surprising coming from a former science advisor to the British Government. Cox managed to restrain his anger, but it was obvious he was annoyed that King – the head of a body that champions the progression of science – should be negative about something drawing physics and science into the headlines. For someone on a mission to bring science into the mainstream conversation, he saw the LHC as a perfect metaphor for his life's work and why he wanted people to recognise its importance. 'The LHC has captured the public imagination,' he wrote in the *Daily Telegraph* in the week of the switch-on. 'Which is wonderful because scientific exploration on this scale is a prerequisite for our survival as a species in this dangerous and challenging universe and yet a significant fraction of the population would usually rather watch *The X Factor*. It would be a shame if the ultimate result of billions of years of nuclear alchemy in the heart of billions and billions of suns were considered by the majority to be a pattern of atoms called Simon Cowell.'

Unfortunately, neither Cox nor his colleagues had much time to revel in their success. Just nine days later, an electrical problem occurred, causing the LHC to break down. 'What we know indicates there was a faulty connection between two cables joining two magnets together that warmed up to the point of melting and that resulted in helium being leaked into the tunnel,' said CERN media liaison James Gillies at the time. The resulting repairs would take longer than expected and it wasn't restarted until over a year later, in November 2009.

Luckily for Cox, the media and the public at large had already cottoned on to the scientist from Oldham, who had become ubiquitous during the run-up to the switch-on. He was written about in glowing terms in various papers, with David Smith in the *Observer* remarking: 'Cox became the acceptable face of physics last week. To Cox himself fell the role of public oracle and making unfathomably complex science accessible to the man in the street via BBC2's *Newsnight*, Radio 4, Australia's equivalent of *Friday Night With Jonathan Ross* and countless other media. Cox is poised to slip the surly bonds of geekiness and become the god of small things.'

He was now 40 years old, a successful scientist and part-time television presenter on the cusp of reaching the next level of fame. First up was another *Horizon* in early December 2008. *Do*

You Know What Time It Is? saw him explore a concept dear to his heart. As someone who never wears a watch, he didn't like knowing the time and considered the titular question stupid. Nevertheless, his love of Einstein and fascination with the idea of what we consider to be the fourth dimension meant it was a subject with which he had a lot of kinship. During the making of the show, he met the Earth's Director of Time Dr Dennis McCarthy who spends his career monitoring the planet's rotation for slight changes which alter the atomic clock – so-called leap seconds – and discovered a day is never 24 hours. He also visited Mayan temples in Mexico, where they built temples to time. After getting sunburnt when his director made him stand outside on the previous programme and speak his piece to camera in Chicago, he wore a scarf – this time he wasn't taking any chances. Still, he found something to complain about: those darn creepy crawlies!

Joking that it never specifically stated in his contract that he wanted a room which didn't have poisonous insects in the bath, he said: 'We decided to come somewhere that was riddled with scorpions. Don't ever say you don't get value for money from your licence fee because when we make things, we have to stay in hotels that have scorpion in the bath.' Somewhat surprisingly, the Beeb came in for another spot of jovial battering as Cox berated the trend for documentaries on the network to employ self-shooting presenters. He thought them poor and was pleased that the BBC had hired a proper cameraman to make his programmes look good. The desire for his films to be aesthetically pleasing as well as informative was something that stuck. Audiences enjoyed *Do You Know What*

Time It Is? while critics continued to praise him as a presenter. Reviewer John Beresford noted on *TV Scoop* how different he was to the usual scientists on television: 'With Prof Cox we've got someone younger and less eccentric and as such, a bloke who you would love to go for a pint with so he could blow your brains out with weird scientific and philosophical ideas.'

Joking that Cox lives just up the road from him and so that pint may come sooner than he thinks, Beresford rounded off his review by saying: 'This was, by miles, the best science show of 2008. In fact, this is a show I'll talk about for years to come, no doubt. I feverishly sent texts to friends to make sure they catch this on iPlayer. It was a phenomenal piece of television that has left me completely ga-ga. In Prof Cox, we've got a new and friendly face of science on TV. What a guy and what an astonishing television programme.' It would be hard to top that, but before the end of the year, Cox managed to squeeze in another *Horizon* programme, *Can We Make A Star On Earth?* Searching for a future energy source – that of nuclear fusion, as seen in and used by our sun – he travelled to some of the most ambitious fusion experiments around the globe. This included a bomb-testing facility in America, access to the world's most powerful laser and a trip to South Korea, where he had the opportunity to go inside the reaction chamber of K-Star, the world's first super-cooled, super-conducting fusion reactor.

Crossing the planet, seeing his media profile soar and witnessing the switch being thrown on an experiment he had dedicated several years of his life to, 2008 was a good year for Cox. And there was good news at home, too. Gia had been hard at work, tapping into her geeky side by working on web materials for the sci-fi sequel *The X-Files: I Want To Believe* and *Indiana Jones and the Kingdom of the Crystal Skull*. She was also pregnant for the second time. On top of being a stepfather, Cox was to have a child of his own. He saw the scans and described them as 'amazing'. Now they were living in a house in south London that was a little too small for them.

Gia reached her second trimester by Christmas and Cox bought her an iPod Touch as a present. For a tech-savvy mum-to-be it was the best present she could have received. During her pregnancy, she used it to listen to hypnobirthing sounds as she fell asleep and as her due date approached, she began watching birthing videos on YouTube while lying in bed at night. When labour came, she downloaded the Labor Mate app, which timed her contractions. 'I can't tell you how incredibly useful this little application was,' she said. George Eagle Cox was born around 1.20am on 26 May 2009. Cox was present at the birth, holding his wife's hand as she squeezed it incredibly hard in return.

'Saturn 5' by the Inspiral Carpets was the first piece of music little George ever heard. The song that had turned Cox's mind towards the moon landings (and provided a good singalong) seemed highly suitable. 'We thought, what would be appropriate for his entrance into world?' said the new dad. 'He's already got the swagger.' George's ornithological middle name was, of course, given to him because it was the name of the lunar module for *Apollo 11*'s mission to the moon.

At nine days old, the newest addition to the Cox family was falling asleep after *Newsnight* and waking up every four hours.

Cox was spending as much time as he could with his son because he was on a break from filming *Wonders of the Solar System*. So busy had he become, he needed to book time off from the BBC to witness the birth of his first child. Just three weeks into George's life, Cox had to jet off again to continue filming. It was hard, both for him and for Gia. She herself found it particularly tough. 'It's a LOT harder to have a newborn when you are almost 40 than when you are in your 20s,' she wrote on the website Parentdish less than a month after the birth. 'My newest son, however, seems to be taking after his daddy and enjoys a lie-in.'

There were some problems, though. George didn't seem to be feeding properly and after calling in a lactation consultant, he was diagnosed with a posterior tongue tie. This meant the piece of skin connecting the tongue to the bottom of the mouth was too short and so he couldn't move his tongue in the way that it was supposed to, which made breast-feeding tricky. Gia took him to London's King's College Hospital and after a brief procedure, George was back to normal. She started co-sleeping with him. While Moki had been an easy baby, she described George as 'much more needy'. 'I've been almost completely on my own with him,' she wrote in September 2009. 'My husband is off travelling the world, filming a huge series for the BBC, so I've been single-handedly doing everything – from dealing with a very needy and difficult baby to dealing with my nearly-a-teenager and running the house.'

Nevertheless, as she waited for Cox to return home ('one of the big things on my mind is s-e-x,' she said), George was an endless joy. 'I want to enjoy this little guy as much as possible,' she said, ''cos I suspect he may be the last baby I have.' When Cox was back in London, he certainly did his fair share of parenting – and was sometimes in for a bit of a surprise. '[George] did spend a few minutes with his dad in bed the other morning whilst I made breakfast,' Gia wrote, 'and covered our bed in poo, but that was a lesson for my husband to learn.'

As George grew and began to sleep through the night, the couple suffered as any new parents do. Gia was blunt about the lack of sex as their son reached eight months, positing she didn't want them to create another little brother or sister. Pleasingly for his dad, the science gene appeared to have been passed on. 'He plays with plugs and wire a lot so he's definitely heading down the engineering track,' Cox told *The Big Issue*. 'He doesn't want his toys, he wants switches and remote controls.'

There was a very good reason why Cox was away so much during his wife's pregnancy and the early life of his first son. It was called *Wonders of the Solar System*. But this epic BBC science show almost didn't happen – at least not with Brian Cox. 'He almost didn't do [it],' revealed commissioning producer Cassian Harrison at the Sheffield Documentary Festival. 'Even at the BBC, we had our doubts.' At the same event, Channel 4's head of science, David Glover, admitted he had been approached about using Cox as a presenter, but had said no. 'I'm reminded about it at least five times a day,' he laughed. It's not surprising he is remorseful but Cox himself explained how difficult it was to get the concept off the ground. '*Solar System*, if you go back a couple of years, was a difficult thing to get commissioned,' he said, 'because people, even at the BBC thought, are people really interested in space? Are they *really* interested? And now after the success of the programme, you think it was obvious, but at the time it wasn't. It was a risk and it paid off, I think.'

Indeed, *Wonders of the Solar System* became one of BBC2's most-watched (and talked about) factual programmes in recent times with an average of 4.8 million people watching each week, including 5.3 million for the first episode. It also went on to become a worldwide hit, broadcasting on the Science Channel in America (where Cox appeared on culturally-significant chat shows such as *The Colbert Report*), as well as Australia and Austria, where it was retitled *Geheimnisse des Lebens* or *Secrets of Life*. Its success culminated with a win at the 2011 Peabody Awards, one of the world's most prestigious prizes for documentary filmmaking. So, what was the secret of its success? 'It was below the radar,' explained Cox, as he recalled the beginnings of the programme. 'It wasn't formulaic – it was a new way of making a science documentary.'

In fact, it wasn't all that new. For starters, Carl Sagan had done a similar thing 30 years previously on *Cosmos*. He had been very aware of trying to make something that would have a legacy since radio waves beaming television programmes across the globe that bounced off satellites would be the most likely thing any alien neighbours might see. Cox had had such a large-scale series in mind for some time but the timing had never been right. 'The kinds of things we started out writing were big, huge, landmark, massive science programmes,' said Gia, re-iterating their *Apollo's Children* idea. 'Travelling all over the world – one minute, you're on the Amazon and one minute, you're in the desert. We took these around [to commissioning editors] for years and years and years. If you think about what science on TV was like 10 years ago, everyone's like, "this is too big, we don't do things like this. Think really, really small." And we kept saying no, we're thinking really, really big. And of course no one's going to do something like that with two unknown people.'

But by 2009, Cox was a minor TV celebrity and the BBC sensed a surge of interest in science. They decided to go all out, spending millions on a five-part series, which would be spectacular and universal yet the concept was remarkably simple: send a qualified presenter around the world to show how the laws of physics exerted on our planet are the same as those in the depths of space and how we can understand the universe by examining the natural wonders in front of us. With his easy-going manner, ability to explain complex scientific data in plain language and just as importantly, his ready-for-primetime look, Cox seemed like a straightforward fit.

As a new raft of younger factual hosts such as Alice Roberts, Marcus du Sautoy and Dan Snow took over from the old guard, Cox slotted in nicely. He still saw himself as a research scientist rather than a television presenter. In an interview not long before the show was broadcast, he told me that he was working on an academic paper. 'I'm writing a paper at the moment about measuring Higgs couplings at the LHC,' he said. 'I think you've got to keep your hand in.' As had been the case with *Sunshine*, getting the chance to make *Wonders* gave Cox an opportunity to reflect on what science really meant to him. 'Over a period of time, you're kind of forced to think about what it basically is you find interesting,' he told me. 'Everybody began being a scientist with some kind of connection to the subject. They found it fascinating, in a simple way. With practice, you remember what it was. I hope in the series, we've tried to do that – to go back to the most wonderful bits that you could connect to most.'

The show was divided into five topics: *Empire of the Sun* charted the history of the sun and its influence over every aspect of our Solar System. *Order Out of Chaos* examined orbits and how the randomness of space is actually very organised. *The Thin Blue Line* explored the atmosphere and climate, while *Dead or Alive* looked at how the laws of nature can mean death for one planet and keep another alive. The final episode was one close to Cox's heart and was dubbed *Aliens*, following life to the extremes of temperature and environment on earth and explaining how survival within those extremes might mean life out there in the depths of space. There was an over-arching mantra for the series – 'We live in a world of wonders, a place of astonishing beauty and complexity. We have vast oceans and incredible weather; giant mountains and breath-taking landscapes,' he said. 'If you think that this is all there is, that our planet exists in magnificent isolation, then you're wrong. We're part of a much wider ecosystem that extends way beyond the top of our atmosphere.

'As a physicist, I'm fascinated by how the laws of nature that shaped all this also shaped the worlds beyond our home planet. I think we're living through the greatest age of discovery our civilisation has known. We've voyaged to the farthest reaches of the Solar System. We've photographed strange new worlds, stood in unfamiliar landscapes, tasted alien air.' He was pleased to have finally got the chance to really attack the audience with his take on science. *Horizon* was all well and good, but occasional one-off documentaries were nothing compared to a primetime BBC2 series and he wasn't afraid to admit it. 'There's always an agenda with my stuff,' he said, 'I have an agenda. It's to really celebrate exploration – I really believe that just sitting with our eyes focused on the ground is detrimental and dangerous to our civilisation. I think we have to lift our eyes up to understand this wider environment. I keep saying it throughout the series: our environment doesn't stop at the top of our atmosphere, it genuinely extends obviously to the sun. You need a Solar System at least to allow life on earth to evolve and flourish. It easy to connect with environmentalism, shall we say, celebrating nature when it's on the surface of the earth, but it's equally as important to explore that wider universe.'

And explore he did. Filming the shows required an epic journey around the world and back. For *Empire of the Sun* alone, he travelled to India to watch a total solar eclipse, visited the Chilean Desert, strolled through Death Valley carrying an umbrella, watched the Aurora Borealis in deepest Norway and sped down the river in a boat beneath Argentina's Iguazu Falls. The money – and there was certainly a lot of it – was right up there on-screen. Epically directed almost like a feature film and with a soundtrack to match, nary a scene of the programmes was complete without some special effects or a helicopter shot. Or several helicopter shots. His trademark delivery was in evidence as he talked of the solar eclipse as if it was a moment from *Close Encounters of the Third Kind*, with the Solar System coming down to grab you by the throat, proving we're all just balls of rock rotating around each other.

What was particularly noticeable about the series was how obvious it was that he hadn't visited most of these places before. Describing scenes and areas of pivotal importance in the world of physics, he was as childlike in his witnessing of them as any of his audience might have been, only serving to show how lab-based he had been up until that point. For cynics who argued about the price of the Large Hadron Collider, *Wonders of the Solar System* might have been a more relevant bugbear. While undoubtedly spectacular and beautifully photographed, some of the locations could be perceived as slightly spurious, whether heading to Tunisia to demonstrate how the earth turns on its axis, or spending more time in Hawaii than the cast of *Five-O*. That said his passion was unflinching and infectious, as are many of the facts he relayed with laid-back precision. It's not hard to understand why an audience would relate to him. Teamed with some of the directors he had worked with on his earlier programmes, Cox had carved a niche for himself as a presenter. Much of this was to do with how he spoke his pieces to camera, which always seemed personable and direct, even when he was standing somewhere incongruous.

'I tend to adlib a lot,' he said. 'Fortunately, with the group of people I've got at the BBC, it's pretty flexible so we've got this very loose way of doing it. Which is unusual for big budget – there's always an element of control that people want. I don't really believe in scripts, to be honest! It's a different way of working and it's quite high-risk for the BBC, but they fortunately trust me and the directors now. I hope that comes across, it's a looser feel. You can't sit in White City in London on a drizzly day and write those things. If you're in Death

Valley, with the sun beating down, it just crossed my mind that this guy did it with a tin can, worked out how much energy the sun gives out. You need the freedom to do those things sometimes because how are you going to get the feel of the place or the emotion that place generates when you're sat in an office in London? You can't do it.'

Fortunately, his directors and crew shared the same vision for balancing a well-crafted image with delivering information. 'The director thought it would look great if I had a black umbrella in Death Valley,' he remembered, from a moment during filming on *Empire of the Sun*. 'It was like, surely you can say something with an umbrella?' For Cox, it was key to be involved in as many aspects of the series as possible, starting with structure. 'The discussion is what should be the structure of the programme and what story should we try and tell?' he said. 'In *Empire of the Sun*, for example, we had two stories. One was the geographic empire, so the edge of the Solar System, and the other one was the life cycle of the sun. We've had loads of meetings and talked about what I think should be in the programmes. Obviously it's such a long process, I can't be on top of everything so what tends to happen is the directors come and say "Well, I've got an idea, I think this would look great on telly," and the things you do are usually suggestions from the director.'

And they made him do some amazing things. Swimming in the sea, off the Baja Peninsula in Mexico, to collect the substance gypsum also found on Mars. Standing beside geysers in Iceland as they shot their plumes of boiling water into the air. Storm-chasing in Oklahoma... But it wasn't all fun. When asked by *Metro* the most difficult location he'd ever shot in, he replied: 'Filming at a volcano in Ethiopia [for *Dead Or Alive*]. It's one of the hottest places on earth. It's spectacular, but you can't work in the daytime because it's too hot. We were in a lava field, miles from anywhere, with no shelter and no water.'

The Erte Ale volcano was certainly tough. They flew in by military helicopter, with Cox complaining it was a dirty plot by the director to make him as uncomfortable as possible. Roped to the edge of the most active lava lake in the world, holding a gas mask and madly coughing, thanks to the sulphur-filled air, Cox still managed to joke about cooking some chips in it. Using the venue as an excuse to talk about Io, Jupiter's closest moon, the crew spent three days in rough tents, battling 50°C temperatures during the day. He bonded with the crew, who spent their downtime reading his first book, Why Does E=mc2?, and teasing each other. He even suggested Erte Ale could be the next holiday hotspot, so long as they built an Irish pub and poolside and bought some sun loungers. For all the accompanying hardships, the series was still an excuse for Cox to experience things he had never done before and he loved it. 'In the third programme, *The Thin Blue Line*, I went up in a jet fighter, up to 60,000 feet in South Africa, which is an old Cold War fighter,' he recalled. 'There were only four in the world flying and now there are three because one of them crashed! I shouldn't laugh, it's the one I flew in – it crashed a month later. They're not the safest of planes, they can take off and fly upwards vertically; they're completely overpowered. It's essentially two Concorde engines with a cockpit on the front. It was just me and the pilot, vertically upwards to 60,000 feet and it emerges upside down because of the way it has to fly up and you see the curvature of the earth and the atmosphere, just the thin, tenuous line of atmosphere that protects us from space. It was absolutely brilliant! You just don't get to do that sort of stuff.'

When the first show was broadcast in March 2010, it was virtually devoured audiences and critics alike. They admired the stunning images and took enough information away from the programmes to impress their friends at the pub; they were also impressed that Cox didn't shy away from the tougher, slightly more apocalyptic elements of the subject, whether the eventual death of the sun or the possibility of asteroids hitting the earth. It was an occasional funereal tone he would return to more frequently in *Wonders of the Universe*. Ultimately, though, it was the presenter himself who garnered the most praise. While some reviewers chafed slightly at sections of the series such as the elongated introductions designed to keep the viewer watching, almost like an advert, none of them could fault the man presenting it.

'Quite a lot of viewers love Brian Cox too, I guess, because he bridges the gap between our childish sense of wonder and a rather more professional grasp of the scale of things,' wrote Tom Sutcliffe in the *Independent*. 'And even if you can't entirely suppress the suspicion that this series exists, not because the BBC urgently felt that cosmology needed addressing, but because they needed to find something for Brian Cox to do next, as a primer in cosmic dazzlement it works very well indeed.' Sam Wollaston in the *Guardian* wrote with almost crush-worthy awe of the opening episode. 'It must have been a Eureka moment for whoever discovered him, as he's very good,' he said. 'And not just because he's totty, with a nice, soft Lancashire accent (steady!). But because he clearly feels a huge amount of love and wonder for what he does and he talks about it all in a way that you wouldn't necessarily expect a physicist to talk. Cox's romantic, lyrical approach to astrophysics all adds up to an experience that feels less like homework and more like having a story told to you. A really good story, too. Who knew that the sun had seasons, or that when clumps of hydrogen collapse under their own gravity, a star is born? Is that how Cox came about, I wonder. Oh God, this is pathetic, I'm clearly smitten.'

Cox himself had a slightly less self-absorbed reason as to why the shows struck a chord. 'What made *Solar System* so attractive were the astonishing new images coming from Casini, the probe orbiting Saturn and all the discoveries from the surface of Mars,' he told *C21 Media*. 'Since the BBC had last made a documentary about the Solar System, we've had rovers all over Mars, discovered ice there and water on Europa. These are all new discoveries. The past decade has been a golden age for discoveries about the Solar System that hadn't been put on TV in that way.'

Cox and the programme-makers were pleased at the success of the series, though none of them could quite believe the scale of it. 'On the one hand, it's pleasantly surprising,' said his friend and colleague Professor Jeff Forshaw, who consulted on the series. 'But on the other hand, Brian's brilliant at what he does and I always felt the appetite's there, that people want to understand science. It captures people's imagination – Brian's exploiting that.

In a sense, I'm not that surprised and it's really encouraging. I think very often there's a danger of dumbing down the way that science is presented to the general public out of fear it's too difficult and that people won't understand it. I think that's not as true as people might think. The basic ideas, I think people are really receptive to it and I think that's what Brian's demonstrated with these wonderful programmes he's made.'

In the aftermath of *Wonders of the Solar System* being broadcast, there was one moment that made him realise he had stepped up to the next level in terms of visibility and therefore critical debate by viewers and other interested parties. It was thanks to an offhand but what he described as a 'factually correct comment' about astrology, which triggered a bit of spat between himself and some of the more mystical viewers and the BBC. In the show, he said that astrology was gobbledygook, but some of the audience didn't like it, triggering outbursts across the Web and spawning several complaints to the BBC. So, how did he respond? 'The BBC asked me for a statement and I apologised to the astrology community for not making myself clear,' he said. 'I should have said that this new age drivel is undermining the very fabric of our civilisation. That wasn't issued by the BBC complaints department.'

But for a man who was still very much a professional academic at heart, the incident threw up some intriguing new dimensions as to the way he thought about presenting. 'Television doesn't have the same aims as science. Science is simply the process by which we seek to understand nature. It is utterly apopulist,' he said. 'In other words, when it comes to the practice of science, the scientist must never have an eye on the

Top and Bottom Left: The celebrity professor signing the accompanying book to his BBC series, October 2010.

Bottom right: As the science expert on *Looking Good Feeling Great* with co-host Fern Britton in 2006.

Pictured proudly showing his OBE awarded for services to science in October 2010.

Top: At the Edinburgh International Television Festival in 2011.

Bottom: The stars of the Radio 4 programme *The Infinite Monkey Cage* at The Times Cheltenham Science Festival in June 2010.

Top: The man of many faces, beside the 'digital chandelier' at Manchester Science Museum.

Bottom right: At the British Comedy Awards with comediennes Jo Brand and Sharon Horgan in January 2012.

Presenting an award at the 2010 BAFTAs.

Top: Applauding the success of participants at The Prince's Trust and L'Oreal Paris Celebrate Success Awards with Prince Charles.

Bottom: With his increasing celebrity status the professor opens Manchester Science Museum's new 'revolution Manchester gallery'.

Top: Posing for pictures at the Edinburgh International Book Festival.

Bottom left: Another day, another award ceremony for the professor at the RTS Awards 2011.

Bottom right: Pictured excitedly leaving the Radio 2 studios.

Top: Cox in his element at the 2011 Telegraph Hay Festival.

Bottom: Smiling for the cameras once again at Edinburgh's International Book Festival with Mariella Frostrup.

audience for that would be to fatally compromise the process. Now contrast that with television. There are customers, viewers, reviewers, consumers, so television must reflect to a certain extent the majority and minority views of the population. But what if the majority of the population doesn't share the scientific view? What if the findings of science run contrary to deeply-held beliefs? What if the accepted scientific position might offend some viewers? I think, however, there are potential problems with broadcasters assuming a totally neutral position in matters such as this. Not particularly in trivial cases like my spat with the astrologers, where it's clear that perhaps discretion was the better part of valour, but in areas of real import. This illustrates a real point of friction between the scientific view and the imperative for the broadcast to remain impartial whilst allowing the presenter or programme-maker to offer a view.'

He was becoming increasingly aware of the balance he had to tread as a mainstream BBC presenter and the responsibility it entailed with millions of people literally believing what he was saying, whatever that might be. Indeed, a 2004 MORI poll of adults over 16 suggested 84 per cent of them gained their information about science from what they saw on TV, on the news or in documentaries like his. He was particularly sensitive about being misconstrued, as he perceived some of the scientific stories in the news to be. One particular bugbear was the furore over the MMR vaccine, which had come under suspicion after being linked to autism in children. Cox thought it was ridiculous and bristled at the way it had become a genuine story.

'For some reason that utterly mystifies me the practice of vaccination against disease has itself become controversial, yet the control and eradication of certain diseases through vaccination is arguably the greatest of all human achievements,' he told the audience at the 2010 Huw Wheldon Lecture. 'The classic example is smallpox, which was eradicated in the mid-1970s through a vaccination programme. Until that point, it had killed almost 300 million people in the 20th century alone.' He couldn't understand why people had latched on to the story, which he felt wasn't borne out by the data. 'And here is a real clash between broadcasting and science, because controversial means different things to a scientist and to a broadcaster,' he added. 'In science, we have a well-defined process for what is mainstream and what is controversial and it has nothing whatsoever to do with how many people believe it to be true or not. It's called peer review. Peer review is a very simple and quite often brutal process by which any claim which is submitted for publication in a scientific journal is scrutinised by independent experts whose job it is to find the flaws. Only when they are convinced there are no errors in the experimental procedure or the theoretical reasoning can this paper be published – this is how science proceeds and it works. This is the method that has delivered the modern world. It's good. It doesn't necessarily mean that the current scientific consensus is of course correct, but it does in general mean that the consensus in the scientific literature is the best that can be done, given the available data.'

He then quoted left-wing American anchorman Keith Olbermann, who lambasted certain parts of television's obsession with impartiality. In what might be construed as a knock against the conscientiously balanced BBC, he echoed Olbermann's edict that this was 'worshipping before the false god of utter objectivity'. In trying to be completely neutral, said Cox, it was easy to end up being more opaque. 'It is recognised you can't give air time to every contrarian on the planet, but there are areas which for television are clearly controversial,' he argued. 'Areas in which there is a high level of public debate for example, such as genetically-modified organisms. Therefore I contend that controversial in science broadcasting should be defined in the same way that it is in science, that is a controversial view is not one that runs counter to public opinion, but one that runs counter to the current scientific, peer-reviewed consensus. This means that the most objective and therefore impartial presentation of a so-called contentious story, such as MMR, climate change, astrology or even the so-called evolution debate is to give significantly more weight to the scientifically peer-reviewed position because this will leave the audience with the more truthful view of the current thinking. We're dealing with issues like the life and death of our children and the future of our climate and the way to deal with this is not to be 'fair and balanced', to borrow a phrase from a famous news outlet, but to report and explain the peer-reviewed scientific consensus accurately. So for me, the challenge of the science reporter in television news is easily met: report the peer-reviewed consensus and avoid the maverick eccentric at all costs.' Yes, things had certainly changed and this wasn't something he had had to deal with when he appeared on *This Morning*.

Though proud of what he'd achieved, even Cox himself was slightly thrown by the level of attention now focused on him. As a rock and pop star, he had become used to female attention, but now that dissection of his looks and handsomeness was spreading across the internet and brought up at every interview. When I asked him about his heartthrob status, he laughed, arguing: 'It's one of those things you can't change, what you look like. I'm not particularly vain. Making the series, it gets harder and harder to make them because it's just week after week in more and more unpleasant conditions and in the last one, I look like I've been in the jungle for a year! Completely unshaven, just don't give a shit. The last thing we did was in this cave in Mexico with these life forms which secrete sulphuric acid – like *Alien*! – and it was full of mosquitos and bats, and you wouldn't say [I was a hunk] if you saw that. You'd just see this gradual falling to bits.' But he would have to get used to the love. 'The challenge is not letting that success bother me,' he added. 'There's no point doing that again so let's do something else.'

Something *else*? Music to the BBC's ears, who were so delighted with Cox's efforts that they had already started developing a new project even before *Wonders of the Solar System* hit screens. In my interview at the time, he only hinted at what this might be as he prepared to head off for shooting the following month. 'It's called *Universal*,' he said. 'It's about the universal nature of the laws of physics. We can talk about black holes and the beginning of the universe and the end of the universe, quantum mechanics – all the more esoteric stuff. The same style as *Solar System*, so we want to go to spectacular places and use places on earth to explain these things that are happening, but it's a bigger challenge in a way because there's not as much geology, it's more real cosmology. But we're going to have a go.'

And the results would be even more spectacular than imagined.

CHAPTER 9

MEGASTARDOM

When you're as hot as Brian Cox, it would be foolish to stick to one medium. *Why Does E=mc²?* was released in hardback in July 2009, but began to pick up in profile and sales once it the paperback came out and the first *Wonders* series had made him a television star. The title was a question Gia had asked and her husband realised it might make an interesting book. He suggested it to Professor Jeff Forshaw, a close friend and confidante, as well as his partner in academic papers. The aim of Cox and Forshaw's book was pretty explanatory: explain why Einstein's most famous theory – that of relativity – is true and then examine what it means for the universe. As the introduction observed: 'Difficult as it may sometimes seem, science at its heart is not a complicated discipline.' This philosophy underpinned the book – the aim was not to use any mathematics harder than Pythagoras' Theorem (which was explained) and while application was required, this was a book for everyone.

The style of writing often echoed Carl Sagan. At the beginning of Chapter One, they wrote: 'Perhaps you picture space as the blackness between the stars as you turn your gaze toward the sky on a cold winter's night. Or maybe you see the void between earth and moon sailed by spacecraft clad in golden foil, bedecked by stars and stripes, piloted into magnificent desolation by shaven-headed explorers with names like Buzz.' The book became a popular science bestseller and was nominated by the Royal Society as one of the science books of 2010. It made the shortlist, with the judges saying: 'It's the most famous equation that exists but few people actually know what it means. This book could change that – it's beautifully written and not afraid to tackle really challenging physics.'

The work received rapturous reviews, most of which highlighted the universality and lack of ego. '[It's] clear, sparkling in places and totally without vanity, anyone with an adventurous mind should be intrigued by what two smart physicists say about it in plain language,' said *The Huffington Post*. '[A] delightful little book.' They garnered praise from celebrity quarters too, reiterating how Cox had entered the mainstream consciousness. 'I can think of no one, Stephen Hawking included, who more perfectly combines authority, knowledge, passion, clarity and the powers of elucidation than Brian Cox,' wrote Stephen Fry. 'If you really want to know how Big Science works and why it matters to each of us in the smallest way then be entertained by this dazzlingly enthusiastic man. Can someone this charming really be a professor?' But while all this was pleasing, Cox in particular must have been ecstatic at one plaudit, which came from Ann Druyan, barely known to the general public, but to him a heroine because of her work in co-writing the *Cosmos* television series with Carl Sagan. 'Cox and Forshaw take the equation that all of us know and few of us understand – and make it crystal clear for all of us,' she said, carefully noting the contribution of Cox's fellow scribe and collaborator. 'A thrilling experience of passionate comprehension.'

He couldn't put a foot wrong, it seemed. In the 2010 Queen's Birthday Honours List, Cox was awarded an OBE for his work in promoting science. The announcement came as a bit of a shock, despite receiving the British Association Lord Kelvin Award in 2006 for a similar feat. 'It was a complete surprise,' he admitted. 'I totally 100 per cent didn't expect it. I really am chuffed because it's a nice honour, but more than that, recognising that promoting science to the public is an important thing will hopefully encourage more people to do it.' This may have been a subtle broadside at the scientists who snidely criticised his style of academics and foray into the public domain but it could also have been an admission that while he might not produce any more great research work, there was a definite purpose to his scientific career. After all, he admitted: 'It's still unconventional to have a relatively large part of your academic career spent in public promotion.'

Going to Buckingham Palace was a blast. Dressed in a top hat and tails, he was joined by his parents. 'My dad hadn't been to London since before I was born,' said Cox. 'It was literally in the Fifties, the last time he went to London.' At the ceremony in

October 2010, he was pictured grinning and holding his medal in the courtyard. Afterwards they went for lunch and spent the day sightseeing. For his parents' generation, the chance to visit Buckingham Palace in an official capacity was almost incomprehensible. Perhaps the only negative was that Cox thought his grandfather would have loved the opportunity to attend – 'If I could have chosen one thing to happen, it would be that my granddad would have been able to come to that,' he said.

Nevertheless, he couldn't quite believe it when the Queen asked how the Large Hadron Collider was doing. He replied it was progressing well. Amid all the fanfare, he was typically self-effacing, though. 'This is a wonderful accolade for me personally, but credit must also go to the University of Manchester and the Royal Society as well for allowing me to pursue these projects,' he said. 'Many employers would not have gone so far to support me, or could have made it hard for me to have the freedom to do the TV work, but the university has been totally supportive. I could never have dreamed when I was a student here that I would be receiving such an important honour as an OBE. Every time I receive an award or honour such as this, I feel as though it is further recognition of science. I feel there is a need to take science more seriously in this country and hopefully we are beginning to turn around the public perception. This is a fantastic way of promoting science and I am delighted to accept the honour.'

The fame that had followed the first series was just as unexpected. Already he had been voted onto the list of *People* magazine's Sexy A–Z (under 'Q' for 'Quantum Physicist'), but he now began to get spotted – or rather stared at – in the street.

'Someone said to me once that it depends what channel you're on as to what shop you can't go into without people coming up to you,' he told journalist Rebecca Hardy. 'If you're on BBC2, you can't go into Waitrose. If you're on BBC4, it's Selfridges.' Gia, too, found it strange when women came up to talk to her husband in the supermarket (for the record, their usual was Sainsbury's). 'The only thing she doesn't like is people staring,' said Cox. 'She's not the kind of woman who wants to put make-up on and straighten her hair when she goes out, but she's decided she can't look like she's just got up.'

Milinovich herself was more blunt, writing on Parentdish: 'I'm a scruffy bugger. I'm usually in jeans, my hair tied back in a messy ponytail. These days when I go out with my husband for a walk or a coffee, everyone stares at us. Suddenly, I've started to feel very self-conscious. It won't be long before "they" start talking about what a frump my husband is married to. So, now along with looking after both the kids, doing all the shopping, cooking, laundry, etc., I've got to put on freakin' make-up and wear something vaguely "nice" to go out of the house with him. If only to avoid having to read something about how I look "twice as old" as my husband.' But it would only get worse.

Even far away from home, Cox was being recognised. 'We were filming in the middle of Oklahoma somewhere, just nothing there and we drove past a petrol station and we went in,' he said. 'And we were buying, like, wine gums and the cashier said to me, "String theory. I've got a question about string theory." He didn't even say hello! This was in the middle of Oklahoma.'

He was away from home to film the next series. The name had been changed from *Universal* to, unsurprisingly, *Wonders of the Universe* and was due to be broadcast in the spring of 2011. There were only four episodes this time, four hours of science-based, yet philosophical programming which looked at some of the fundamentals of mankind's existence. The spectre of Carl Sagan loomed even more in his approach this time around. 'Cosmos was on TV in the UK when I was 12, in 1980,' he told The A.V. Club, 'so that would be the perfect age for a kid who is into astronomy anyway, as many are. And to have that series capture your imagination at that age, it makes an indelible impression on you. I think one of the reasons that Sagan is still relevant today and one of the reasons he's very relevant in television, is that his shows were partly polemic. They were not simply – as is the fashion today – these kinds of presentations of what we know and don't know about the universe, which is exciting and spectacular, but there's more to it than that. There's an agenda. Not to science, but to him – he had an agenda. He thought he would build a better world if everybody understood the value of the world and behaved in a scientific manner; he really believed that. He was passionately involved in that perspective and that perspective is not that we're very small or insignificant.

'To Sagan, the perspective was that because civilisation is so rare in the universe, then our rarity could have value. Stepping away from the earth, observing our existence on earth and putting our place in the universe in its proper context, for him, should make us on the planet behave in a more sensible and rational way. He recognised that we're a village. I agree with that. [*Wonders of the Universe*] has that approach; it has message in it. It tries to contextualise these discoveries as well as present them – and why not? In the UK, I am quite political. I work at university and I am involved in the political process. I lobby really hard for funding and support for scientific and engineering programs because I feel that those are the ways that we will progress as a civilisation and as a country. That's what I share with Sagan's view, that you can be an activist – a scientific activist – and you should be able to do that on television and in books.'

Filming was just as tough as before with expansive locations, lots of time spent away from home and large concepts to try and disseminate. Each episode took between four and five weeks to shoot, which meant he was away for 20 weeks throughout the year. Though he had more leverage to increase his free time and spend it with his wife and children, his schedule was an exhausting one. 'You should see some of the outtakes,' he told the *Daily Telegraph*. 'They have one outtakes film which is just me swearing. Five minutes. It would be great to get it out there, but the BBC would never allow it.'

They had to wait a week at the beach in Costa Rica to capture footage of giant turtles crawling out of the sea to lay their eggs and an ambitious experiment in Brazil, though scary to shoot, ended up being highly satisfying. 'Something that really worked was the prison demolition sequence in Rio,' he remembered. 'We used it as an analogy for a collapsing star, a star at the end of its life that has run out of fuel and it collapses under its own gravity. It does that in a matter of seconds, on the same timescale as a building collapses when you detonate it.

Wandering around a building that is full of live dynamite and explosives is not very relaxing! It was all wired up and ready to go but when we blew it up, I thought it really worked well and I enjoyed it a lot actually, as a television piece.' Not everything worked, though. 'We had a catastrophic time filming in Bolivia,' he explained to Shortlist, 'so catastrophic, in fact, that the particular section didn't even make it into the series. We all got altitude sickness, it's very unpleasant to shoot at 5,500 metres. Truthfully, *Universe* was much more of a challenge to make than *Solar System*.'

Despite the rigours that went into making the four shows, he felt they had come up with something that he and the BBC could be proud of. 'It's the [show] I wanted to make,' he said. 'I've got a good relationship with the production team at the BBC. I don't know how to make films but I have a clear view of what I want to have in them. If it was down to me, I'd force the content level up too high, but they need to make something accessible and beautiful.' He was very conscious of trying to keep the show grounded, despite its lofty themes and the fact that it discussed locations many millions of light years away – not exactly accessible on a BBC budget. They had dazzling graphics, but he was keen to reiterate that this was not just a big CGI fest.

'The ambition of the series is to try and get away from using too many graphics, if possible,' he said. 'You obviously have to use some graphics because we are talking about quite esoteric concepts, but we tried to put these things "on earth" by using real physical things to talk about the processes. What we did, we went inwards into the prison and at each layer, we said here's where the hydrogen fuses to helium and here's the shell where helium goes to carbon and oxygen, and another shell all the way down to iron at the centre of the stars. That's the way stars are built, so we used this layered prison to illustrate that and then collapse it. That's a good example of what the ambition of the series was.' This was demonstrated in the first episode. 'I like to use simple things,' he explained, 'so in the first episode, I used a sandcastle, literally a sandcastle, to explain something. The posh name is the second law of thermodynamics, but to us it's everything falls to bits eventually.'

Though grand in scope, the four *Wonders of the Universe* shows came down at their heart to simple ideas. The first, titled *Destiny*, was one of the more downbeat opening episodes to a science series, explaining the end of the universe and life as we know it through the theories of entropy. While eager not to repeat himself, the basic structure remained the same as *Solar System*: long intro, lots of epic time lapse photography and helicopter shots, as well as the camera concentrating on Cox experiencing all this in a personal context. It was, as he had laughed about during the making of his 2008 *Horizons*, all about a journey.

The second episode was called *Stardust* and examined many of the ideas he had shared with the makers of *Sunshine*. It was its own kind of creation story, explaining how humans were made among the stars. Part three – *Falling* – revisited a familiar topic. Accompanied by a Bobble Head toy of Albert Einstein, Cox explored his predecessor's Theory of Gravity. To finish, *Messengers* discussed light and used photon energy as a conduit into the Big Bang. As a series, it was cleverly put together, starting with the end of the world and working backwards. With its portentous title and apocalyptic outlook, *Destiny* saw Cox traverse from an abandoned diamond mine in the Namibian desert (the scene of the sandcastle) to a Patagonian glacier. An ancient temple in a far-flung corner of Peru made him think of home, only in the sense that he joked about building a similar kind of solar calendar-based edifice in his back garden. The word 'profound' got a thorough workout, as did long establishing shots of Cox staring into the distance or at some impressive sight.

Stardust was more upbeat, with lots of interesting take-home knowledge. Travelling to Kathmandu to observe a Hindu cremation ceremony may perhaps have been overdoing it, but Cox's explanations of how the Himalayas are essentially made from long-dead and crushed sea creatures (in the limestone) were fascinating, as was the knowledge that all the gold mined in the world would only ever fill three Olympic-sized swimming pools (which seems rather far-fetched).

He also got to indulge his playful side, blowing bubbles to illustrate nuclei joining together and throwing sodium in a bottle of water until it exploded – a childish experiment that made him giggle. The Rio prison demolition sequence was suitably filmic, a style that was repeated through the series. Though aesthetically bombastic, in a science documentary (and not *Spooks*), it felt a bit silly, as did an action movie-style montage sequence while he prepared to step into a centrifuge à la James Bond in *Moonraker* in *Falling*. Managing to accelerate to 5G before he cut it off, emulating the gravity he would have faced on some of the universe's exo-planets, this was the only thing that managed to make the professor appear actually older than his years, an experience he described understatedly as 'quite unpleasant'.

The final show, *Messengers*, spun history all the way back to the Big Bang. 'Understanding the universe is like a detective story,' he said, and that's how he approached it, going back through the evidence that led scientists to understand light from billions of years ago. He travelled to Tanzania to take a photo of the Andromeda Galaxy and looked at rainbows over Victoria Falls in Zambia. At Carnak Temple in Egypt, he watched the sun rise on the morning of the Winter Solstice, just as the Pharaohs had done, 2,000 years previously. Whether breaking the sound barrier on a Hawker Hunter jet fighter, or examining some of the oldest fossils of complex life ever discovered in the Canadian Rocky Mountains, this was the apotheosis of what the *Wonders* series was all about: big theories, large numbers, the sun flaring into the camera lens, projectors on a deserted African savannah, extravagant set-ups, B-roll sequences that resembled a French film from the 1960s, poetic language; also grand, if something non-sequitur-style music – and Cox at the centre, a benevolent presence laying out what it all meant for the audience and the world around them.

As the final clip of him kayaking solo down a large river faded over the credits in a shot almost designed as a hero image, the BBC had clearly found their saviour of science and they were already bolstering his star power. Along with his production team and the BBC Science unit, he had achieved a perfect example of understanding the modern viewer and what they want from a show of this type. 'The trick, of course, is finding the most effective contemporary means of delivering this message and this is not, as a physicist would say, time invariant. In other words, the techniques of television change with the years,' he said. 'It's always tempting to gaze backwards to an imagined golden age, probably the television you watched when you were ten or twelve years old and bemoaned the inevitable evolution in presentation and editorial style. But for me, the most visceral connection with an audience is achieved when a programme or presenter moves beyond a presentation of the facts and figures, and places the scientific discoveries in their magnificent context. The presentation of ideas must sit at the heart of great TV.'

Ratings for *Wonders of the Universe* went through the roof. Each episode was repeated two days after the first showing and the first episode was watched by an incredible 6 million, an extremely high figure for a BBC2 factual programme. The first showing on Sunday nights, for example, received over 4 million – over double the amount something in the same timeslot usually gets. By the end of the series, it was averaging between 5 and 6 million viewers per week, almost soap opera numbers. The reviews were mainly as rapturous as for *Solar System*. 'His scientific account of the cyclic nature of the cosmos is an immensely fascinating one, and was especially enlightening to those who wondered just *how* we know the chemical makeup of astral bodies from unimaginable distances, and Cox explained this in just enough detail without bogging the theory down with overly indulgent sci-babble,' said Den of Geek. 'Again, Cox's practical illustrations of his points were inspired and over the course of the hour, we visited geysers in the Chilean Andes and a Brazilian prison, which was utilised in what must be one of the most satisfying demonstrations of a dying star in educational history. Was it really necessary to show Brian walking away from the explosion in slow motion like an astrophysical Keanu Reeves, though? Only the director (who clearly has lofty ambitions) can answer that, and tropes like this may be the price we have to pay for a programme that does, admittedly, once again look superb. And by the time the hour was up, Cox had explained with commendable clarity and enthusiasm the life cycles of the stars themselves. Fascinating stuff, once again, and Cox imparts these facts with such a love of his subject that you hang on every word.'

Others, while still heaping praise on the presenter, had a bone to pick with certain sequences. 'What is it with the BBC and mountain tops?' wrote Tom Sutcliffe in the *Independent*. 'Is there supposed to be some hint at Mosaic inspiration here? Either way, it's become tediously predictable and it should stop. And it's particularly unforgivable when you have a presenter, such as Cox, who is actually capable of drawing you in without being marooned on an icy pinnacle, with a BBC safety officer having kittens somewhere just out of shot. *Wonders of the Universe* is an attempt to take advantage of the success of Professor Cox's previous series, *Wonders of the Solar System*, which unexpectedly spun out of low-earth orbit to find a substantial general audience. Like its predecessor, it's big on cosmic dazzlement and mind-boggling perspectives and full of epic orchestration and screen-saver graphics, most of which are much less successful at conveying the immensity of the ideas involved than one human being talking to you directly. It helps that he doesn't go too deep. But the point of such programmes is less to explain every detail than arouse a generalised sense of awe that might spin off into further thinking, and Professor Cox is very good at that.

'When he tells you that a photograph of an unremarkable red blob in a field of fuzzy white blobs is "one of the most interesting images taken in recent astronomical history," you're inclined to believe him, or at least give him time to explain why. And the final sequence – in which he outlined the unimaginably distant moment when the last star gutters to a cinder and "nothing happens and it keeps not happening for ever" – conveyed a genuine chill of mystery.' Sam Wollaston in the *Guardian* didn't so much review the programme as write a comedic faux diary entry by Cox himself, pointing out his glamorous wardrobe and way with huge numbers. And Chris Harvey in the *Daily Telegraph* outlined how rare was a presenter of Cox's ilk, with the seemingly effortless ability to stop confused viewers wanting to switch over. 'The explanation for why time always moves forward required Cox to make plain the second law of thermodynamics,' he wrote in his review. 'The first law, as we all know, stipulates that when a TV scientist tries to slip the phrase "second law of thermodynamics" into a sentence, a large proportion of viewers start wondering what's happening on *MasterChef*. Cox is different. Scientists who can capture the popular imagination come along extremely rarely. Those that are also photogenic enough to look good striding along a deserted beach or gazing at a glacier are even rarer.

'The most poetic sequence was probably the one in an abandoned diamond-mining town in Namibia. Founded in 1908, after a single diamond had been found in the sand, it had long been abandoned and was gradually being reclaimed by the desert. Cox used it to explain why the world doesn't run in reverse, with the help of a sandcastle that he made with bucket and spade. It was an almost perfect snapshot of the combination of academic science and childlike wonder that Cox provides.'

Ultimately, that was what made the shows so successful – a mix of stunning images and Cox's unique ability to explain complicated ideas, executed without patronisation, allowing the audience to understand but also feel their way through some of the deeper material. 'My personal view, particularly when communicating complex ideas, is that simplicity of explanation is probably best,' Cox argued. 'In my programmes I feel that I can bring the audience with me on a complex scientific point if I sit down and explain the science as best I can. I also believe that the practice of trying to say absolutely nothing that the audience may find remotely difficult is simply wrong. For me, it's far better to leave the audience with a few questions rather than have them led by the hand gently through a concept and then repeat that concept again to them in a slow, deep voice in voiceover and then repeat it again in vision just to make sure. If in doubt, my view is it's better to credit the audience with too much intelligence rather than too little. Challenge your audience a bit and they respond. This is certainly true in teaching and lecturing, so why shouldn't it be true in TV as well?

'It's my view that the true beauty and therefore the attractiveness of science is only available when it's presented accurately. How can it help the audience to truly understand and appreciate something if you skip over necessary information in the misguided cause of simplification? Science is compelling, but only if you have the facts in front of you.'

One of the perils of a high-profile show is that while you reap the rewards, you also become open to more criticism. Most of this was angled not at Cox himself, but the way the programmes were put together. Much of it emanated from less high-profile peers, who while happy he was bringing science to the mainstream, still had reservations about the format of the show. 'Grumpy old cosmologists (i.e. people like myself) who have watched [the series] are a bit baffled by the peculiar choices in location – seemingly chosen simply in order to be expensive, without any relevance to the topic being discussed – the intrusive (and rather ghastly) music and the personality cult generated by the constant focus on the dreamy-eyed presenter,' wrote one blogger. Another said: 'Television companies and/or commissioners of programmes like to pad out science documentaries with material such as pictures of landscapes, images of the presenter, fast-moving computer graphics and background music. I'm sure that Brian Cox would prefer to be able to make programmes without so many of the less relevant additions, but media culture would make this difficult on mainstream channel.'

Cox in turn addressed the attacks on style over substance, saying to Discovery.com: 'The thing I learned – because I'm interested in two things really, music and science – is that when I make TV programmes, I'm not only interested in making a show that has a lot of scientific facts in it. Obviously I want there to be a scientific narrative and I want people to understand things about the universe but I like to make programmes that look beautiful, for example, where the music works in the programme. So I have a dual interest in making something that looks nice, that's a piece of film really, as well as a lesson. It helps [that I've got a musical background too], because I have an aesthetic appreciation of what I want to do.' He was unapologetic, adding: 'It is my view, the best way to use television to build a more scientific world is to make TV programmes that celebrate science, that present the facts accurately to be sure, but also place upfront the beauty, emotional power and profound implications of the scientific worldview because science is, at its core, a deeply human pursuit. It stems from that most human desire to explore and explain the world around us.'

Not everyone agreed. For many viewers, one particular sticking point was the volume of the background music by Sheridan Tongue, a freelance composer who scored both series. BBC's *Points of View* revealed that 118 complaints had been made to the Corporation, saying the music made the narration impossible to hear. One person wrote: 'You don't have to dumb everything down by pretending we're all in a nightclub.'

Wonders executive producer Jonathan Renouf bowed to public pressure and reduced the volume, saying: 'There's enough volume of complaints over this. I think we clearly have made an error of judgment so we are re-mixing the sound for all of the films, to pull down the music and effects levels when Brian is talking.' Cox was furious at the BBC kow-towing to what amounted to a small minority, arguing: 'It should be cinematic experience – it's a piece of film on television, not a lecture.' But several disabled charities praised the move. A spokeswoman for the Royal National Institute for the Deaf said: 'RNID welcomes the BBC's decision to lower the level of background music on the *Wonders of the Universe*, which will make this already dramatic and engaging programme more accessible and enjoyable for people with hearing loss.'

With hindsight, Cox was slightly more amenable to those who might have a problem with the way the programme was shot and suggested there would be a rethink before embarking on the inevitable follow-up, which had tentatively been titled *Wonders of Life*. 'I accept some criticisms of the series,' he told interviewer Stuart Jeffries. 'I think the days of standing alone on a mountaintop while a helicopter circles round me are over. We're not going to do that again. But it's a challenge to suggest the epic, awe-inspiring nature of the universe. When Carl Sagan made *Cosmos*, he got a lot of stick. So do I. But it's hard: how do you keep the body of the documentary and remove all the visual clichés? To be honest, I'm a little bored of the grandiose thing and I want to move on.'

In fact, viewers were already comparing him favourably to his idol, especially the younger ones. 'Brian Cox's presentation style is right on for a large fraction of the under 25s,' wrote teacher Rhodri Evans. 'I find the style of the programme superficial compared to *Cosmos*. But, last year I showed the opening ten minutes of *Cosmos* to my students and I could see from their faces that many had switched off. Carl Sagan's eloquence is too verbose for young people of today, 30 years on. My 14-year-old son would also find *Cosmos* too ponderous, but loves *Wonders*.'

Not only was the series a smash hit, but so too was the book accompanying it. The BBC had used the same vehicle with *Wonders of the Solar System* and liked texts to appear in Tesco and Waterstones alongside their flagship shows. Co-written with BBC commissioning editor Andrew Cohen, it even reached the top of the non-fiction charts. Cox was especially happy. 'You know what I'm pleased about?' he said. 'It displaced One Direction's biography because it's gone from One Direction and now it's a physics book. I love One Direction – great band – but it says something about culture, doesn't it?'

And the reason why Cox and Cohen's tome had gazumped the *X-Factor* group was because it didn't follow the easy route of simply being a parade of pictures from the programmes. 'Traditionally these books are quite coffee table, image-heavy books,' said Cox. 'The filming of the series took longer than we anticipated, so actually the book got written relatively quickly because I had time to sit down and just really write about the physics. Although it is tied with the television series, it does go quite a lot deeper in many areas. I'm quite pleased about that. So it's more than just snapshots of my view of the physics of the TV series. I should say also, some parts of it are in the form of a diary of what it was like filming the TV series. There are always some things you do and places you go that have quite an impact on you. And I tend to take a lot of pictures, so many of the photographs in the book are mine.'

The success of *Wonders of the Universe* sent Cox's popularity into the stratosphere. 'There are lots of people who are famous in physics, but famous to a couple of hundred people,' laughs Professor Patrick Regan, a nuclear scientist at the University of Surrey. 'He's a phenomenon, I suppose.' Other high-profile scientists also praised him. 'Brian has made more people enthusiastic about science than anyone in a generation,' said Professor Jim Al-Khalili, a fellow BBC presenter and academic, who invited Cox to talk about his life and career at a University of Surrey debate. 'Today he is a huge celebrity and rightly deserves all the plaudits he is currently receiving.'

He even received a nod from the Astronomer Royal, Professor Sir Martin Rees. 'As an astronomer I'm lucky to work in a subject where there is already public interest and where it's not too difficult to convey the key ideas and new discoveries in a non-technical and accessible way. It's far harder to make particle physics accessible and interesting. Brian Cox is one of the few scientist who succeed in doing this and I much admire him for it.'

Professor Regan points out how hard it is for an academic to connect with an audience. 'A lot of scientists are not very good at doing that media stuff,' he observes. 'They don't want to do it. They're afraid to talk to journalists – they're afraid they'll say something wrong. But it may be with his background as a performing musician, having been involved in that performance industry in another part of his life, helped him feel comfortable in the presentational aspect of what he does.' But with the ubiquity and fame, it was sometimes difficult to remember Cox was first and foremost a driven academic. 'I met him once in a professional sense,' recalls Regan. 'He was on a funding committee. I chatted to him briefly about science. The Science and Technology Facilities Council (STFC), they're the funding agency in the UK for particle physics, nuclear physics and astronomy. It's effectively the government pot, which underpins fundamental research in the UK – you put grant applications in to fund your research. Brian Cox was on the PPRP; it's a project panel and their job was basically to evaluate whether a piece of equipment was worth funding or not, so that's how I met him. The committee he was on, there were about 15 or 16 people on it. There are no idiots on [the committee]. To be on those funding council committees, which is part of our peer review, I think it's fair to say you have to be a respected scientist in the field: you're there to evaluate the quality of other people's research proposals and in order to do that, you have to be pretty good at research yourself. There are lots of other people who are very good particle physicists, but he'd be in the elite group of people in his age [group] in the UK.'

Even Regan concedes it's hard to maintain a presence as a television presenter and research scientist, though. 'I think probably there's two bits to his life – one is a professional scientist and he's a professional presenter,' he says. 'He is a media and TV phenomenon and I suspect he's reasonably well-remunerated for that. I think you probably do have to give up some of the science because of the time pressures. I don't think it makes the presentation any less valid.'

Requests for his time, while previously extensive, now became impossible to manage. 'In a way that's Brian's problem. He is really nice and he wants to do everything,' said Gia. 'He gets asked to do talks at schools ten times a week and he doesn't have the time – but he wants to do them. He's trying to work out a way of doing that; he's really keen on outreach and reaching people who aren't necessarily already interested in science. He wants to reach new people and get them interested in science.'

And she didn't mind exploiting her husband's sex appeal either. 'I'm particularly interested in reaching kids and girls,' she said. 'And teenage girls love Brian and it's so awesome! We went to the Edinburgh Science Festival a few years ago and Brian did a couple of talks there and it was all old men, basically. The last one we went to, he did some talks and it was all, like, 16-year-old girls – that is really cool. Fine, it's teenage hormones, but they're getting interested in science and use what works!'

Indeed, Cox's looks had become the subject of many articles and messageboards. Eleanor Mills in the *Sunday Times* dubbed him a 'floppy-haired piece of intellectual crumpet'. On the Digital Spy forums, hundreds of threads opened to discuss and dissect his handsomeness. 'I have a whopping great crush on the man,' wrote one. 'I haven't had a full-on celebrity crush for a while, so I am focusing all my crush efforts on poor Brian.' Another called him a 'Galactic Dreamboat', while some (male) bloggers thought he looked young for his age. With fame came the slightly peculiar posts, too. 'As a hetero male, I would,' said one, while another added: 'I wonder if he can change a plug and put an IKEA chest of drawers together?'

Someone else wrote: 'I think it looks like he is smiling when he talks because of the shape of his mouth and the size of his teeth. I don't think he can help it. It is a bit distracting but I still listen to him.' Above all though, they marvelled at Cox's ability to explain science. 'I absolutely adore the prof!' explained coolmum123. 'He is crazy intelligent but explains things so well they actually make sense. I wish he had been my physics teacher, I would definitely have enjoyed it more!!' Meanwhile,

Sparkle added: 'I think he's great. It's very tough to find the right level on a show like this and there will be some people who already have good knowledge of the subjects, who will find flaws, and people for whom it's still a bit too much. However, he and the production team seem to have found a level that is working for the intelligent, but non-expert general public.' One woman decided mere comments were not enough, though. On the One Hand Clapping blog, she created a poem-cum-lyrics about him: 'Oh, Brian Cox, Brian Cox/Let us dance beyond Orion's rocks/Please hear this, my heartfelt petition/You can be my personal physician/You're so steamy, so D-Reamy/I wish that we could form a teamy/Oh, Brian Cox, Brian Cox/You're my favourite science fox/My love for you is spilling over/Please stop, before I turn supernova.' And those were merely the last three stanzas! It's hard to know whether it was tongue-in-cheek or totally serious.

Though Cox said he was not presenting on television to be famous, that didn't stop him from agreeing to appear on a number of well-known TV shows. He sat on the panel of *Would I Lie To You?*, was interviewed by Jonathan Ross, lent his expertise to *QI* and even got to sit alongside one of his childhood heroes, Sigourney Weaver, on the sofa of *The Graham Norton Show*. He joked about his appeal to teenage girls on the CBBC show *Dani's House*, appearing in a dream sequence where he talked of building a Dugong Collider (dugongs are large sea mammals) and smashing the animals together to produce a delicious substance known as 'sea cheese'. He travelled to America and appeared on the satirical politics show *The Colbert Report* (he first appeared in October 2009 and returned in July

2011), where he got on really well with the presenter, Stephen Colbert, and was impressed by all the pictures of Saturn hanging in his host's office. He even showed up on television when he wasn't actually on TV – as an impersonation by Jon Culshaw on BBC's *The Impressions Show*.

Personally, he was impressed. 'You know what I like about it?' he said. 'They usually descend into Liam Gallagher when people do impressions of me and he's stepped back from that, so it's a bit more gentle.' Ricky Gervais, however, was slightly more perturbed by the caricature but only because it spoilt how the comedian saw Cox. 'That's terrible now, because I think [Cox] is a genius,' he declared. 'But now, when [Culshaw] puts in those little bits of poetry, it's done now.'

Perhaps the strangest thing for Cox was simply how everyone seemed to want to talk to him and to ask him questions; he even signed a fan's plaster. Some people would approach him on the street and shout something out about black holes, rather than engage him in a discussion. 'It's really nice when fans want to come up and want to have their photo taken with you,' he said, 'but it's not just one or two people anymore. It's 20, 30, or 40. It makes it virtually impossible for me to go shopping. At the moment, I'm just eating takeaways because I can't go out to Sainsbury's.' He was aware of how abnormal it was. 'It is unusual, because I am basically an academic,' he said. 'And for an academic to present some TV programmes and to get 6 million viewers and people asking for your autograph, it is different. I suppose that this is the first time a scientist or documentary-maker may get his picture in the *Sun*. It's just a difference of image, really.'

His old friend Chris Evans suggested jokily they should market a Cox-branded range of telescopes. Around this time, his musical background came back into focus. A tabloid story came out stating he had turned down the chance to appear on an album sleeve for Scottish band Belle & Sebastian, with keyboard player Chris Geddes saying: 'This band's going to break up over Brian Cox.' Cox responded to the fiction on Twitter, writing: 'I'd have been on their album cover – they never bloody asked!'

It was also announced in March 2011 that he would be returning to the stage as a musician. British Sea Power were to participate in a gig alongside The Flaming Lips at Jodrell Bank Observatory and Cox tweeted he would be on stage with the former band. All 5,000 tickets were snapped up, with a spokesperson revealing: 'Professor Cox is going to play keyboards with British Sea Power. It's a great idea and obviously quite fitting that he plays at Jodrell Bank, given the television programmes he's making at the moment. He will be learning some of the songs from their set but, who knows, there might be some D:Ream stuff as well.'

Unfortunately, Cox had to pull out of the concert, thanks to a timetable clash. It's no surprise, considering how frenetic his lifestyle had become: voted 11th Most Influential Man in Britain by *GQ* magazine one minute, being asked if he was interested in an *X Factor* for scientists the next. The participants of The 38th Annual Saddleworth Beer Walk paid tribute to their local hero by going on a pub crawl wearing Cox face masks and calling themselves The Brian Cox Appreciation Society, donning T-shirts with slogans like 'Particle Physics gives me a

Hadron' and 'Prof says I will do science to you'. He was even mistaken for his namesake, the Scottish actor whose credits include *Manhunter* and the *Bourne* franchise.

'I once booked a car to the airport with the same firm used by the actor,' he told *Metro*. 'The driver picked me up at 6am from a different address to the usual one and until I showed my face, he thought the other Brian Cox was having an affair.' Ironically, before he found television fame, Cox wasn't even the most well known 'Professor Cox' at the University of Manchester. Professor Brian Cox was also an Emeritus professor of English Literature at Manchester and was celebrated in his field as a scholar before he passed away in April 2008. He has since been usurped on Google.

Yet while it may have seemed easy to lap up all this adoration, there is always a downside to fame. And it wasn't manifested in the inability to buy some oranges from the supermarket either. He told the *Daily Mail*: 'The other day, a woman came to the door and said, "You're on the telly, aren't you?" I said, "No, I'm not. Goodbye." And shut the door.' Perhaps more profound was when Gia Milinovich wrote a much-debated article in the *Guardian* titled: 'THE LADY VANISHES: INVISIBLE WIFE SYNDROME'. It caused something of a furore on the comment boards and she wrote a similar piece for Parentdish. There, she described an incident at one of her husband's public appearances. 'We attended a screening of one of his programmes to a sold-put audience,' she wrote. Having seen the show itself, Gia simply attended the Q&A afterwards. 'Our son luckily fell asleep in my arms just before the screening, so slept peacefully during it. The moment it ended, however, he woke up. As my husband sat down on stage, our son shouted out, so I left the auditorium and spent the next hour sitting with my son in the exit stairwell. And all I could think of was what a perfect analogy it was.'

She received lots of messages from other women who felt the same way – successful, intelligent women who were married to someone who became famous, whereupon they themselves entered a strange kind of existence. 'It's the experience of a lot of women,' said Gia. 'And I'm interested to hear the experiences of men, if their wives are well-known.' She was accused by some of whininess and jealousy despite carefully wording her article so that she wasn't perceived as being something she wasn't. And she acknowledged that her husband's success meant they finally had enough money for her to live a more comfortable life, without having to worry about rushing back to work after giving birth to George. More than anything, though, she seemed to find it baffling. 'I have no problem with [his fame], I don't care, I'm not jealous and that's some of [the] things I think people thought from my article,' she said. 'It's more actually in a personal situation, the way that I suddenly find people react to me in a different way because of who my husband is, which I find really bizarre. So it was nothing to do with the work that we've done together or anything like that. I'm very, very happy.'

In fact, it was other people and the way they reacted when Cox came into a room that caused the difference. 'Before he was known by the wider public, we might go to a dinner party where we didn't really know anyone and people would talk to me like I existed,' she continued. 'I was a person and I had people asking me about my interests, and we'd have a conversation about politics or whatever. Now, often I'm just kind of standing there and nobody talks to me and I'm starting to think about what's the point of actually going out of my house? It's not an unusual experience. The other thing that has started to happen is people will say "Oh well, you only think that because your husband's a physicist" whereas before they wouldn't have known who my husband was. Now suddenly I'm incapable of having my own thoughts because they know who my husband is. That's a bit rubbish, actually; it's a bit insulting. I've found myself in this kind of role, which isn't necessarily what I wanted when I was 25 years old. I'm a feminist woman, and independent and all that stuff but sometimes you have to think about the wider picture and what it is that you're trying to achieve.'

It must have been particularly difficult considering how rarely Gia actually got to see her husband Even though he was able to negotiate a bit more time at home between and during filming the big series, his increasing workload in the UK was almost undoable. She admitted having rarely seen him in the past two years. 'He's back for six days, but every single day he's booked up with something,' she revealed. 'It's not been easy. Of course he wants to see all these amazing places around the world and that shouldn't be ignored. On the one hand, it's an amazing experience. On the other hand, it's really, really hard. Judging by the response that I had and the emails I got from people, it's not unusual – it's not an unusual situation for a woman or a man who's married to someone that suddenly finds fame to experience this really strange existence.'

The attitude of the naysayers annoyed those who knew and respected Gia Milinovich. Fan Sara Webb met her on a number of occasions. 'She came across as a very funny person; great sense of humour,' she says. 'Very open and straightforward, she is not shy in stating her opinions and I thought she came across as smart and articulate.' Still, she understands the internet can be a dangerous place. 'I hate to say it, but I think there is a *lot* of bitchiness about Gia,' she explains. 'I've seen it and it makes me angry, as she has been a lovely person when I've met her. I've seen her unnecessarily criticised for her appearance because she is not someone who will deliberately plaster herself in make-up every time she ventures out of her house. People on the internet, who don't know her, seem to write her off as some bit-part in Brian's life despite the fact that she has been his rock for many years and is the mother of his child. People can be very spiteful.'

Instead, Webb was impressed by the strength of Milinovich's character. 'Definitely her intelligence, her sense of humour and her love for her fella (she never shuts up about him),' she says. 'She was saying how proud of him she is, and mentioned him a lot when we were talking – but not in a "show-off" kind of way, if that makes sense. I got the impression that they are very close and secure in their relationship.'

Meanwhile, Cox's partnership with his friend and colleague Professor Jeff Forshaw hadn't been left in abeyance. Forshaw had been a series consultant on *Wonders of phe Universe* and by October 2011, they were ready to unveil their second book together. *The Quantum Universe: Everything That Can Happen Does Happen* was released at the end of that month. As they saw it, quantum physics was one of the fundamental theories lay people should try to understand, not only because of its contribution to the study of science, but also real world applications like solar panels and the laser, neither of which would have been discovered if not for quantum physics. Their trademark approach to science writing was still intact. In Chapter One, 'Something Strange Is Afoot', they wrote: 'Quantum theory does, admittedly, have something of a reputation for weirdness and there have been reams of drivel penned in its name.' Though the conversational tone in the latest book was prevalent, so too was the barrage of information and facts. At the beginning of the second chapter, they explained: 'Ernest Rutherford cited 1896 as the beginning of the quantum revolution because this was the year Henri Becquerel, working in his laboratory in Paris, discovered radioactivity. Becquerel was attempting to use uranium compounds to generate X-rays...' Their latest book had been harder to collaborate on, thanks to Cox's hectic international schedule this time around but somehow they had got it done. The publisher described it as a 'brilliantly ambitious mission to show that everyone can understand the deepest questions of science', before adding: 'This is our most up-to-date picture of reality.' Certainly, Forshaw believes it is for everyone: 'We tried to write a book which actually takes people through by the hands from the beginning and explains, step by step, what quantum physics is, what it means to say that a particle behaves according to the laws of quantum physics. I firmly believe that if somebody's interested and wants to know about these things, then they can. It's accessible. This is definitely not stuff which is the domain of some bloke in an ivory tower.

'I come from a background where I struggled originally with physics. At school, I found it difficult – I nearly didn't carry on to study physics at university. I feel very lucky that I did do it. I'm not some kind of great intellect. Quantum physics has got a reputation for being difficult because it's very, very counter-intuitive. We're being asked to accept a picture of the world which is in complete contradiction to our common sense. It's nothing like anything we experience in everyday life.'

The two men crafted the book during runs and over rejuvenating curries. 'We like running, so we both go running together,' says Forshaw. 'Brian has a nice place out in the hills near Manchester. So we often go running together, come back, have a curry, drink some beer – and talk. And keep talking and asking questions of each other. And through that process, we unpick our own understanding of the subject.'

Utilising theories such as Richard Feynman's least action/sum over paths with clocks representing phase, they dabbled with Werner Heisenberg's Uncertainty Principle and tried to explain the fundamentals of quantum theory, which is that atoms could – in essence – explore every part of the universe, every second. Forshaw gave a classic example of this to the *Financial Times*, arguing it had taken eminent physicists 20 years to get their heads round the concept, even after important breakthroughs. 'I can throw a ball through the air and we think the ball is kind of moving along some definite trajectory and that it's always somewhere,' he explained. 'But that's not what's happening; every atom in that ball is in a real sense exploring the entirety of the universe at every instant.'

This is where the maths comes in, with probabilities, but

Forshaw says by treating it as a game, it could be taught to children. 'People who have heard of the words quantum physics and relativity are interested in them and a little bit more, and quantum physics probably better than any other branch of physics showcases how wonderful modern-day physics is,' he says. 'You often hear people say how the fundamental theories of nature that we've got these days reveal a universe which is very beautiful, very profound and all these kind of words which hint at something deep. It's deep in that quantum physics does underpin all natural phenomena; it is beautiful. But we both feel that if you really want to understand what that means, then the way to do that is to actually understand quantum physics. Rather than get some vague sense of the ideas, actually understand the content. That's what we tried to do. People get confused because it's so strange; that should be separated from the technical content, which requires very little mathematics. You don't have to be a master of mathematics to understand it.'

With Cox away, it was left to Forshaw to take a first pass at the manuscript. 'The version that I write originally is written for Brian,' he explains. 'I write it at too high a level. So it's a really nice process, it really works. We get to convert it from something that is a little bit too dry, a little bit too formal, and then it gets this process where we're trying to make it more accessible with each iteration. The difficult part is actually getting the structure laid out, getting the ideas laid out and having a clear idea of the material we want to present and how we want to explain it. That's where all the work goes – in trying to find the way to explain it in the simplest possible way. The way it tends to work is I make a first pass and then Brian goes through and completely rewrites it. And then I go through it again and Brian goes through it again. The whole book, there are no joins in it – it genuinely is written by the two of us, back and forth.'

Reviews were glowing, though a couple were not so convinced as to the ease of the contents. Popularscience.co.uk gave a rave review overall, but suggested fans of Cox's television series might be surprised if they picked up his latest literary offering. 'The reason The Quantum Universe will disappoint is not because it is a bad book. It's brilliant. But it is to Cox's TV show what the Texas Chainsaw Massacre is to Toy Story. It's a different beast altogether. As they did with their E=mc2 book, but even more so here, Cox and Forshaw take no prisoners and are prepared to delve deep into really hard-to-grasp aspects of quantum physics. This is the kind of gritty popular science writing that makes A Brief History of Time look like easy-peasy bedtime reading – so it really isn't going to be for everyone, but for those who can keep going through a lot of hard mental world, the rewards are great, too.'

It went against what Cox and Forshaw were attempting when they set out to write the book, even if its mere presence on the bookshelves made browsers think briefly about science. 'Brian and I are really motivated to write these books because we want to communicate some of our love of physics to the general public,' says Forshaw. 'Given what I said before about struggling myself at the beginning, just knowing how easy it is to miss the boat, I feel passionately that if I can help to contribute to helping people understand better the law of nature and these wonderful laws of physics, then it's well worth [it] for me to do it.'

Cox had done documentaries, books and music, but he hadn't considered himself a comedian, at least not professionally. But stand-up and writer Robin Ince had other ideas as he approached him to participate in the next stage of an idea which had really begun back in late 2008. As an atheist, he had created *Nine Lessons and Carols For Godless People*, a Christmastime comedy show loosely based around the subject of atheism and combining top performers such as Ricky Gervais and Chris Addison alongside former Pulp frontman Jarvis Cocker and scientist Richard Dawkins. The project had flourished and Ince now wanted to move on. His solution was *The Infinite Monkey Cage*, a Radio 4 show and podcast which saw the comedian team up with Cox for a 'witty, irreverent look at the world of science'. Each week the pair were joined by guests who contributed songs in case of Tim Minchin, science chat or comedy thanks to folk such as Dara O'Briain and Katy Brand.

'This is a moment of huge enthusiasm for science,' said O'Briain. 'In comedy, there is a big push towards people arguing on behalf of rational thought and great reaction against things that have no basis in reason.' Each episode revolved around a specific topic, such as Christmas or the origins of life. After becoming a hit on the radio, as a natural live performer Ince saw the idea had further potential. 'I wanted for a long time to do spectacular shows about science,' he told journalist James Kettle. 'I believed there was an audience that wanted to come to a show and then leave with a reading list.' The result was *Uncaged Monkeys*, a touring live show featuring Cox, as well as an array of guest stars, depending on which city they were in. The list was impressive – everyone from author Simon Singh and *Bad Science* journalist Ben Goldacre to comic book maestro Alan Moore.

Despite both himself and Cox not believing in God, Ince was quick to point out that the point of the show was not to take a swipe at religion. 'The show's not really about attacking fundamentalism,' he explained. 'It's mostly whizz-bang science, songs and people larking about. It's about celebrating life.' Together, they travelled the length and breadth of the UK, though Cox insisted they were put up in better hotels than when he worked for the BBC. Though he wasn't supposed to focus on trying to be funny, it was a new direction for the scientist, who had previously told interviewers jokes such as 'What noise does a subatomic cow make? Muon.'

Generally, the reviews were positive. 'Cox is a compelling speaker, careful to pepper his lectures with gags at the expense of Large Hadron Collider alarmists,' said the *Scotsman* of a performance in Glasgow, April 2011. 'Currently less than the sum of its parts, *Uncaged Monkeys* nevertheless feels like an important development in live edutainment.'

By the time the tour reached London's Hammersmith Apollo in the December, it was clear to the 4,000-strong audience that the idea had been warmed to. 'Two questions sent via Twitter during last night's interval encapsulated the appeal of pin-up particle physicist Brian Cox,' wrote Bruce Dessau in the *Evening Standard*. 'One asked him if there was a bit of the universe light had not reached. The other asked him to sign a fan's penis.' After Tim Minchin arrived on stage to play his controversial song about Jesus, following which he was joined by Cox for a duet called 'White Wine In The Sun', Dessau suggested: 'In a parallel universe, Minchin and Cox are undoubtedly massive rock stars. They probably feel like rock stars in this one, too.'

For the main duo, the process of trying to combine proper science with comedy was an intriguing experience. 'I have a problem with telling jokes about physics,' Ince told The List. 'Quite often the audience have no idea what you are about and to be honest, I don't know what I'm talking about either.' Cox was quick to reply. 'It depends on the level of your jokes, I suppose,' he mused. 'The famous one-liner about F16 fighter jets, Polish plumbers and singularities in the complex plane, requiring a deep understanding of Cauchy's integral theorem, is probably never going to work. But I do think that a society in which everyone has a basic knowledge of, for example, Newton's laws of motion, Einstein's theories of relativity and quantum mechanics would be a better place to live.'

They held no truck with people who argued about alleged bias towards rationalist thinking, echoing Cox's concerns about reaction to science on TV. 'When we do *Infinite Monkey Cage* on Radio 4, we often rail against the idea of "balance",' said Ince. 'So, someone might say, "Shouldn't an argument about evolution also have someone who believes in intelligent design?" Do you think we could get around that problem by simply saying, "Well, that's one opinion, but now, in the interest of balance, here is someone who is wrong"?' Cox was just as vociferous. 'This would be one acceptable compromise!' he said. 'The problem with today's world is that everyone believes they have the right to express their opinion and have others listen to it. The correct statement of individual rights is that everyone has the right to an opinion, but crucially, that opinion can be roundly ignored and even made fun of, particularly if it is demonstrably nonsense!'

It was clear that the pair were having fun. Life on the road reminded Cox of touring with a band, with some small differences. 'We won't be punching the air or stage-diving,' he explained to *Reader's Digest*, 'but will we be accused of dumbing down science? Yes, of course we bloody will! They'll be sniping, especially the online lot. It's just snobbery. Maybe some people think that, because I'll be sharing a stage with comedians such as Robin and Dara, I'm making fun of science. Not at all! I think there's a very important connection between it and comedy. If a comedian hears someone talking rubbish, he'll tackle that person. If a scientist hears someone say that the world was created 6,000 years ago, he'll say, "No it wasn't! Shut the fuck up!"

'Comedians and scientists are often rational people, quite brutal with their intellect. Ultimately, we're just trying to engage people. I'm trying to advertise science, to say, "This is what it does and this is why it's important to all of us."'

The shows attracted a unique crowd, who were rarely catered for by usual theatre experiences. When asked jokily whether the groupies were still in force, Cox told Shortlist: 'I'll reserve my judgment about science groupies until after the tour. If we all end up being treated like Take That or the Beatles, then I'll know something's up. I'd be surprised, though – we don't exactly look like the Beatles.'

Though Ince's concept, it was another brilliant career move on the part of Cox as he looked to spread his wings. Plus, he got to show off another side to himself. 'There are many Schrödinger's cat jokes,' laughed Ince when asked how the show managed to mine comedy out of a seemingly dry subject. 'Also, Many-worlds Theory allows you to tell one joke and then expound on all the possible different outcomes, which is handy for lengthy stories.'

Many academics might have been flustered being around celebrities, but not Brian Cox. It partly helped he was already friends with many of them but when it came to making appearances on TV chat shows, it was clear that he was comfortable with famous people. Which was lucky, because the BBC decided that the next logical step was to create a show in the tradition of *An Audience With...* and put Cox at the centre.

Night with the Stars was a pun-friendly programme broadcast on BBC2 in December 2011 from the Royal Institution of Great Britain's illustrious lecture hall. In front of a crowd crammed into the heavily-raked seats that included Jonathan Ross, Simon Pegg, comedian Al Murray and *Fast Show* actor Charlie Higson among many others, Cox espoused a lecture on quantum theory. 'It makes me proud to be a scientist in this day and age,' said science presenter Liz Bonnin, as the show prepared to go on air, while *Top Gear*'s James May joked: 'I'd like to ask Professor Brian Cox about his hair – it's a shared interest.'

Backed only by a blackboard, an autocue, a million-pound diamond and some small experiments, Cox led the occasionally baffled audience through some of quantum theory's important points. 'No helicopters tonight,' he laughed, pretending to stare into the distance, arguing his loyal fans would be upset if he didn't do at least one wistful gaze. Instead, this was Cox unplugged, as he got stand-up Sarah Millican to do the double-slit experiment, exploded hydrogen bubbles in May's hands and embarrassed his friend Ross by getting him to attempt quantum mathematics. While Ross joked about Cox's apocalyptic outlook, his host explained how quantum physics predicts white dwarves and introduced Pauli's Exclusion Principle.

The latter even caused something of a furore on the physics Internet message boards, with some commenters on www.physicsforums.com saying he was incorrect. Showing how he still enjoyed interacting with fans – and remained a competitive academic at heart – Cox left his own riposte to the critics, clearing up any misrepresentations and publicising his book at the same time, telling one commenter he would do well to read it because it might mean a better class of degree.

While scenes of Pegg and physicist Jim Al-Khalili waving a spring around as *Red Dwarf* actor Robert Llewellyn looked on made for entertaining pre-Christmas television, the programme also served as an important watermark. For TV show creators, the giving of a Christmas special by the channel is a massive moment: then comes the realisation that you and your characters have become part of the establishment. As far as TV bystanders were concerned, this was what *Night of the Stars* was for Cox: an anointment by his BBC employers as someone worthy of that honour. It was also, thanks to the subject matter, a handy advertisement for *The Quantum Universe*.

When Amazon's telescope sales were reported as increasing by up to 500 per cent after the first night of *Stargazing Live* in January 2012, one might be forgiven for asking Cox whether he would rethink those eponymously branded star searchers, as Chris Evans gamely suggested. After 3.8 million people tuned in for the opening episode of the astronomy programme, it wasn't all that surprising they were thinking skywards. 'Each time [Cox] appears on TV, we see a jump in telescope sales and that would appear to point to a significant "Brian Cox Effect" encouraging a renewed interest in stargazing,' said Neil Campbell of Amazon.co.uk.

It wasn't the first time that Cox and the BBC had attempted something of this scale and showed how ubiquitous he had become as the voice of science for the broadcaster. Here, he was chosen to lead an astronomy-orientated programme even though his research expertise was within the realm of particle physics. He was no doubt a fan of space, but was not a professional cosmologist despite having a cache of knowledge on the subject. To the BBC audience however, his voice was the one they wanted to hear.

The first *Stargazing Live* had taken place in January 2011 at Jodrell Bank in Manchester, with a three-day extravaganza combining televisual output, an internet presence and more importantly, collaboration with various astronomy groups across the country, who were all invited to participate. In other words it was a truly interactive experience. The 2011 series went well, with Cox talking about Jupiter and speaking to the crew of the International Space Station, while co-host Dara O'Briain (who had studied maths and theoretical physics at university) offered insights. The show got the headlines, too when astronomer Mark Thompson (working as an outside broadcaster) told Cox and O'Briain that nothing was happening in the skies over Macclesfield, only for eagle-eyed viewers to point out that he had missed a meteor streaking across the sky. As it turned out, it came from the Quadrantid meteor shower.

More than 40,000 people participated in over 300 *Stargazing Live* events around the country and some places such as the Newbold Verdon Library in Leicestershire had to add further dates later in the month. It was a highly successful regional event and proved the BBC right in their belief that science programming had truly entered the zeitgeist. 'The BBC linked with observatories all over the country to motivate people to look at the stars,' said David Strange, chairman of the Norman Lockyer Observatory in Sidmouth, Devon. 'Our observatory opened its doors to all budding stargazers and offered help and advice about starting an interest in astronomy. We were at our maximum capacity, so were very pleased with the turnout.'

Indeed, 2.4 million people downloaded the *Stargazing Live* Star Guide, making it the most downloaded BBC resource of all time and so it was perhaps a no-brainer for the Corporation to revisit the idea less than a year later in a bid to emulate 2011's audience, which peaked at 4 million viewers per night and ended up being seen by more than 10 million people.

'The Brian Cox Effect is massive,' O'Briain told the *Radio Times*, just before the show was broadcast on 16 January 2012, again the first of three episodes. 'People may witter on about Brian's hair and his dreamy eyes – and he does, of course, have them – but the viewers who are simply swooning over him tend to miss the fact that his programmes are fantastic. Brian has found an audience hungry for something that has substance to it – his programmes have tremendous heft.'

He went on to explain what he hoped people would get out of the new show. 'If they discover one thing that nestles in their head, that would be brilliant,' he said. 'People assume that a lot the things on TV are faked these days but what made the last series for me was that everything was absolutely genuine. In the opening moments of the show, I said to the astronomer at Jodrell Bank, "What have we got?" and he replied, "We've got Jupiter." There was a beat and as I looked through his telescope, I thought, "Jeez, we really have got Jupiter. That's amazing!" That was a genuine wow moment. The planet was actually there, clearly visible through the telescope – it was not filmed in a zoo in Holland!'

Second time around, the show was just as expansive with events up and down the UK, from Scunthorpe (where 20 amateur astronomy enthusiasts collected and pitched their ' scopes in a bid to capture Jupiter and Venus) to a BBC Big Screen in Londonderry, which connected with the Faulkes Telescope project in Hawaii. Even the Mayor of Derry, Alderman Maurice Devenney, said: 'I am a big fan of the BBC's *Stargazing Live* programmes.' A special musical project was attempted, with young people from three major cities working together at Jodrell Bank Observatory alongside a BBC orchestra to take sounds downloaded from the Lovell Telescope and turn them into songs.

Cox was joined by the man who had impersonated him – Jon Culshaw – as well as one of his heroes, Eugene Cernan, the last man to walk on the surface of the moon. The manner in which Cox conducted that interview ('in awe' might be the best way to describe it) demonstrated just how pivotal space travel, and particularly the moon landings, had been to his own development. 'I could have talked to Captain Cernan forever,' he said. 'I've got his phone number now, I'm going to ring him back.'

Meanwhile, two regular guys found themselves at the centre of a excited media storm after they appeared to discover a new planet. Chris Holmes from Peterborough and Lee Threapleton were two of the many volunteers asked by the show to study reams of data on the Planethunters.org website, a page which looks after data collected from NASA's Kepler Telescope. After finding a planet that was around the same size as Neptune, Holmes admitted to the BBC: 'I've never had a telescope. I've had a passing interest in where things are in the sky, but never had any more knowledge about it than that. Being involved in a project like this and actually being the one to find something is a very exciting position.'

The planet was dubbed 'Threapleton-Holmes B' by Cox, who went on to say, 'I think it is genuinely exciting. Fun aside, normal people have found a planet, something none of us could do 20 years ago. I think it's a remarkable thing.'

Stargazing Live 2012 was another hit. Audiences of all ages found themselves drawn into the interactivity of the programmes, enjoying the chance to put questions directly to Cox in the spin-off show, *Stargazing Live: Back to Earth*, in which he joined celebrities like Andy Nyman and John Bishop, as well as fellow scientists Tim O'Brien from Jodrell Bank and space medicine expert Kevin Fong. Cox loved working on this since it tapped into the same sense of wonderment that he himself had experienced as a young boy looking up at the stars. He also got to present a different side of himself on screen. As co-host, he wasn't just a pundit but engaged the guests and addressed the camera, much as he had a decade before during Network of the World.

Once again, he bantered with his employer, revealing that he had to sign a Health & Safety form in case the team discovered aliens during the live show after he had fired radio waves through Exoplanet Kepler 22-b. 'The BBC had to look through its editorial guidelines and see what its instructions were if we did discover aliens,' he joked. Looking back on the experience, he hoped the one thing that people would take away from the show was the inkling to join or set up their own astronomy society. If his sway over television audiences was anything to go by then it wouldn't have been surprising if 100 didn't spring up five minutes after the end credits.

Yet perhaps the most tangible consequence of Cox's influence through his television programmes and public profile is something the media latched on to with glee. 'I have heard people call it the Brian Cox Effect,' says Professor Paddy Regan, a physicist at the University of Surrey. 'That may be true. When I was a kid, I would have had no idea how to [become a professional scientist]. So, having [him] on TV probably helps open people's eyes to that.'

In August 2011, when school leavers around Britain received their A-level results, there were some interesting statistics. Exam board Edexcel saw physics entries rise by 6.1 per cent in 2011, biology entries rose by 7.2 per cent, while maths and further maths increased by 7.4 per cent, as did chemistry 9.2 per cent). Previously, cultural phenomena such as forensic cop show *CSI: Crime Scene Investigation* have been credited with upswings in interests, but was Cox and his series really the catalyst for this apparent surge? 'It could be the Brian Cox Effect,' said Ziggy Liaquat, managing director of Edexcel, while Joe Winters from the Institute of Physics observed, 'While we don't have any hard evidence to show that Brian Cox is the main reason for the resurgence in the popularity of physics, anecdotally we're confident that Brian has been a major driver of increasing interest levels in the subject.'

Cox's belief is that peer-reviewed consensus is the one way to determine whether is a theory is correct but there are others who are not so sure. Imran Khan is the director of the Campaign for Science and Engineering in the UK (CaSE). 'There's a yes and no answer to this,' he says. 'I'll give you the "no" part first. A lot of the reason [why] people have been talking about the Brian Cox Effect is we have seen an uptake in the number of people studying science, maths and engineering at GCSE, A-levels and university over the past few years. And of course at the same time, we've had this fantastic series from Brian Cox. People are sensing an excitement around what he's communicating and thinking, well, surely that's got to be part of the reason why we're seeing this uptake in the number of people studying these subjects?'

In Khan's eyes, though, it's a matter of timing. 'The thing you've got to realise,' he adds, 'is we're seeing an uptake in people taking A-level and degrees in science and maths, and in order to do that, they had to take the right GCSEs and A-levels going back three or four years, so the groundwork which has enabled the uptake we're seeing now had to have started about four or five years ago. And indeed the people we see who work in the sector, say at the Institute of Physics at the National Science Learning Centres, they've been working really hard for the past four or five years to lay that groundwork.'

That said, the jump – particularly in a niche subject like astronomy, which has climbed 40 per cent in the number of people wanting to take it at university – must have come from somewhere. There was even a story of sales of telescopes at John Lewis increasing by 50 per cent following *Wonders of the Solar System*. 'It's difficult to see how you can get a jump in just one year without there being some kind of particular effect. And I do wonder whether Brian had something to do with that and his programmes,' says Khan. 'Generally, the fact that people have been laying this groundwork in terms of making sure schools have the right number of physics teachers and making sure the students know what these subjects get you, it's quite likely that having someone who's seen as charismatic can influence people's decisions about whether they want to take advantage of these opportunities.'

While fans of Cox will never admit his ubiquitous presence could be in any way negative, there are some who though fans of his work, suggest attributing a change in young people's attitudes to science to just one person might be perceived as dangerous. Khan argues it's because the other institutions and government departments striving for this are not given due credit. Professor John Dainton from the University of Liverpool, who worked with Cox when the latter was an undergraduate and often goes out to drum up support for future science undergraduates in schools, offers another potential pitfall: lack of ability.

'For the last two or three years, it's been very clear that the only thing 13-, 14-, 15-year-olds know about science is that they like Brian Cox. They always ask you, "Do you know Brian Cox?" and when you say you know Brian Cox, they say, "How do you know Brian Cox?" So I say, "Well, he was a post-graduate student working alongside me." And they say, "Ooh, aah, fantastic!"' he explains. 'All the things that he's done have made science cool, as they would say. The applications for hard-nosed physical science (which is a bloody difficult career) are going up. People are saying it's sexy to do it. Whether they survive when they ultimately get to university and take on such a course has yet to be seen, but we can see we're getting bright people coming through, wanting to do physics degrees and mathematical physics degrees and astronomy because someone at the age of 13 – when they were 13, it was Brian Cox – said to them it's cool.

'But then sometimes there's a bit of a reaction because it's a long, hard grind. It's like becoming a doctor: you've got to work at it and there are no shortcuts and that in a way is sometimes a bit of a shock to people. It's a damn hard undergraduate degree. Whether they're aware of that when they come into the subject one doesn't know, but at least they're coming into the subject much more than they did.'

CaSE's Imran Khan, while not entirely convinced of the so-called 'Brian Cox Effect', is happy to propagate it as a theory – with caveats, though. 'I don't think it's detrimental,' he says. 'The key thing is the stuff that he does is fantastic and it's a great way to raise the profile of so many things we're interested in. In terms of research funding, he talks about why it's important for the UK to be supporting science and engineering. In terms of people studying it, these are the same aims we have. We're totally aligned there. The question isn't doing down to what Brian's doing because we want more of it, we just need to make sure the media and government realise that as well as that, you need all these other factors in play as well. [But] if it gets young people excited in what science and engineering can offer, then so much the better. It's a really exciting time to be a young scientist – there is a buzz. Going back hundreds of years, science and engineering have formed a really important part of what the UK stands for and if we're starting to regain an appreciation of that, so much the better.'

But he does wish for one particular difference: a female Brian Cox clone. 'Physics is one of the areas and engineering is another where we still have a big gender imbalance so one of the things people have mentioned to me is [that] it's great we have Brian Cox, but where is Bri-ONY Cox? We need a female champion of science as well.'

Still, Cox himself was proud of his contribution, whatever the scale. 'I've heard that admissions into physics are going up at universities,' he said, 'so if that's true and I played a little part in it, then brilliant!'

CHAPTER 10
THE FUTURE

The continued success of every show that Professor Brian Cox puts his name to makes him a rare television beast – a guaranteed hit machine. That's unlikely to change with *Wonders of Life*, the third in his epic series about the most important aspects of our cosmos and how they connect to each other. In March 2011, he expressed a desire to eschew the grand mechanisms of the television series to do a televised public lecture – 'Just me in front of a blackboard about the Theory of Relativity or black holes for an hour.' He almost achieved this in *Night of the Stars*, though the BBC insisted on a celebrity audience rather than a group of average science enthusiasts.

It seems unlikely that he will deviate all that much from his tried-and-tested formula for *Wonders of Life*, which began filming towards the end of August 2011. Described by the production team as a show that is 'looking at the physics that underpins life on earth', he spent three weeks filming in Mexico, arriving during a huge rainstorm. They shot in the Karst Caves in the Yucatán, on the famed Copper Canyon Railway and at a lake outside Creel, home to a microbe whose progenitor was one of the complex life forms that helped to change the world. Cox was up to his old tricks, testing out the polarity of water using a tin can and photographing pond skaters, while the team tweeted about practising other experiments for the programme and returning home with a car boot full of heavy metals and jump leads.

The second episode precipitated a trip to the Philippines, where they filmed in the mountains of northern Luzon. Cox also visited the island nation of Palau, where he travelled to the legendary jellyfish lake to explore the interaction between jellyfish and the internal symbiotic algae. This required him to visit the Brighton Dive Centre before filming, where he qualified as a scuba diver and once the sequence was in the can, he and his cameraman were able to improvise a scene at one of Palau's nearby reefs.

It's safe to say fans of the show will not be disappointed by its scale, even if Cox joked about how he used to scale mountains in a helicopter as he was pictured riding up a trail on a donkey. As one of the BBC's star presenters, however, the relaxed attitude from the network in the previous series now meant Cox and his team were left to do as they wanted. And it was just the way he liked it. 'The BBC gives producers like me an immense amount of artistic freedom,' he told C21 Media. 'I see virtually no top-down interference in the programme-making process. There's guidance, almost always constructive, but basically if I, my director and my exec producer agree on something, we do it; that freedom is very valuable as documentaries authored by professional scientists are the most enlightening and emotionally impactful.

'That's the great success of the BBC – it has this artistic freedom to push boundaries and take commercial risks because they're not commercial risks. If I thought these kinds of documentaries were in decline, I'd be concerned. I don't see any other format that engages people as I was with *Cosmos* and James Burke's *Connections*, where you can develop an idea over six, seven, eight weeks. There are some ideas that you just can't do in one hour and it would be a tragedy if people stopped making these series. For the BBC, as a public broadcaster it would be a dereliction of duty.'

Time will tell whether they'll allow him to include the Lady Gaga song he wanted on the soundtrack, though.

But was Cox still able to call himself a professional scientist as opposed to a full-time science presenter? Of course his eminent research history speaks for itself, as do the honours bestowed on him by the Royal Society and others. American universities offered him jobs and the opportunity to take his expertise to the United States, but with his family and his focus in the UK, he turned them down. However, his hectic broadcast schedule made it increasingly hard to do the 'day job'. 'I'm really lucky because I've got this diverse scientific career now,' he said. 'I started very much in research, absolutely focused in research, but it's kind of broadened out into a lot of public talks, making television programmes for the BBC, which has allowed me to travel around the world, meeting lots of interesting people. Also, meeting a lot of politicians and really arguing the case for universities and for science, which I think is so self-evident you shouldn't have to argue it, but you do.'

As far back as mid-2010, he found himself unable to answer the phone in his university office – whose walls are covered in pictures of the LHC – because of all the fans ringing for a quick chat. Similarly, his email inbox – its address easy to locate on the internet – was unmanageable. 'He's quite rigorous about not replying to his academic email if it's not related to academic stuff,' says former colleague Chiara Bellati. 'You do need to write to him via his agent. With things developing for him, he's being very rigorous about not using that email for anything other than his physics.' Instead, Cox took great joy in coming up with funny out of office messages to annoy his detractors. One read: 'Professor Cox cannot respond to you because he is currently evolving'. He still interacted with both fans and critics too (and often the latter) because he wasn't able to contain himself. When a writer called Roy Stemman posted on his Paranormal Review blog that he was disappointed with a Cox tweet about the non-existence of ghosts, calling him a 'nobber' for implying all those who believed in ghosts were wrong, Cox was quick to retort, describing the article as 'a pile of shit'.

While many students may have applied to Manchester knowing that he was an academic there, logistics meant his presence was minimal, though. 'You never see Brian Cox around because he's always off doing stuff,' says one student. 'Obviously he has to put his research on hold because of the fact he's off promoting physics in the media, which is fair enough because it needs to be done. And it works obviously. But you don't see as much of him doing research or giving lectures.' Despite his absences, he continued to be a strong public advocate for tertiary education. 'They're important because they take kids and move them out of their home town, mix them up with ideas and other people and a bigger world,' he told *The Sunday Times*.

Luckily, the Manchester physics department is packed full of people exactly like Cox – young, thrusting professors who are experts in their fields and keen to pass their knowledge on. Jeff Forshaw is still a constant presence at the university and while he doesn't consider himself a rock star, he can measure the impact of the work he has shared with Brian Cox on the younger generation. 'I think the students know me now,' he says. 'A lot of them have read the first book and I've been on the telly a few times. It's good. Manchester's physics intake is burgeoning; we're completely rammed full. I'd like to think a part of that is the contribution that Brian and I have made to popularising science. I wouldn't want to take too much credit – we've got two guys who won the Nobel Prize!'

Forshaw and his friend planned more books. 'We've got one or two books we're thinking about,' says Forshaw. 'It's not decided yet, we need to talk about it with our editor. I like the idea of writing a book about how old things are. So there's going to be another one, that's for sure.' For Forshaw, it seems like a long way from the days spent drinking and laughing in Hamburg but even he couldn't have foreseen the success his friend would achieve or the path their careers would take. 'Absolutely not,' he insists, 'not for me, anyway. I don't know if Brian had a secret plan but he never mentioned it. This really is a result of loving physics and wanting to communicate it, wanting to talk to people about it and just going with it, really. And recognising that there is an audience for it.

'It was never part of a long-term plan, although both of us are definitely on something of a mission because if I do this kind of thing alongside my research, it's going to take time out of my research, time out of my teaching, so it has to be worth it; there has to be a reason to do it. Struggling myself at the beginning [of my scientific learning], just knowing how easy it is to miss the boat, I feel passionately that if I can help contribute to helping people understand better the laws of nature and these wonderful laws of physics, then it's well worth it for me to do it.'

While it may have become a many-headed beast that none of the department could have fathomed when he first joined the faculty, great affection is obviously held for their famous colleague among the academics. At a department open day, held in the Schuster Building and the Rutherford lecture hall (named for Ernest Rutherford, who they call 'Uncle Ernie' on campus), a picture of a pony-tailed Cox holding his degree was pinned onto the board behind the booth in a collage called 'Life Of Brian' displaying some of his greatest hits in the press – with a round, furry toy stuck to his face like a clown nose. Cox himself explained how his celebrity had helped the university. 'My students are very grateful,' he told the *Sunday Mirror*. 'Before I was on TV, physics students were seen as a bit boring and no one wanted to speak to them. Now they say, "You've made physics cool". The other students are interested in the subject and they get chatted up a lot more.'

Professor Paddy Regan from the University of Surrey reveals Cox's televisual success has helped professional scientists in other ways, too. 'I think more and more fundamental scientists are realising [talking to the media] is an important aspect of what they must do,' he explains. 'I'm sure there are other scientists who would like to be on telly but the idea [that] the world is rampant with scientists who are killing themselves to become TV presenters, that's not true. Ultimately, much of the science we do is funded by the public. I personally think it's very good that science is part of the wider culture and that it's not seen as something weirdos do. Maybe one of the things that's made Brian such a star is 24-hour news coverage. There's lots of channels to fill and somebody somewhere thought it was a good idea to have qualified scientists present stuff, rather than doing talking heads. Overall, that's a good thing.'

Cox still maintains a flat in the Saddleworth area, where he often indulges in a curry at his favourite local restaurant Mitali in Uppermill, but he has become a southern boy, with the main family home in south London. 'To tell you the truth, I'm as useless as I ever was,' he said. '[Physicist] Richard Feynman once said, "A scientist looking at non-scientific problems is just as dumb as the next guy." When it comes to cooking and directions and DIY, I'm definitely as dumb as the next guy.'

Meanwhile, little George went from strength to strength. 'I could easily have not had children, but I'm very glad I did,' Cox told the *Daily Mail*. 'You think before you have them, "Oh, I'm going to lose all my spare time," but then you have them and it's brilliant.'

He dreamed of George growing up in the world's leading

scientific nation. 'I'd love it if George got into science,' he said. 'Gia always says we can never tell what he'll want to do, but he's got a good start and I brought him back a cute space suit from NASA while I was filming in America.' George enjoys watching his father on television but seems to be aware of Cox's television persona, too. Rather than see him on screen and say 'Daddy', he will point and call his father 'Brian Cox'. Cox himself finds this endearing. 'I think it's something every parent can do – find out what their child is interested in and foster that interest,' he revealed to journalist Jenna Sloan. 'I was lucky my imagination was awakened at an early age. If you don't show kids what's out there, they'll never know.'

And he wanted to improve his cooking skills. 'I heat things up as quickly as possible, which is my view of what cooking is, which appears to not be the correct approach,' he admitted in 2010. A year later, he said: 'I love food, I love eating food, so I'm hoping to improve.' He relished his time at home, away from the clutter of public life, and he loved driving despite the London traffic wardens. 'They're absolute hooligans,' he declared. 'They gave us a ticket when we were loading the car outside our house recently.'

He liked the idea of appearing on *Top Gear* and keeps a Sat Nav in the glove compartment of his own car because he doesn't have a good sense of direction (he said he would love to chat to Einstein about coming up with how satellite navigation works). A fan of BMWs, he owned an 118d and was also given the chance to drive a vehicle of the future. 'I did a thing at the Frankfurt Motor Show for BMW – they let me drive a hydrogen-powered 7 series BM,' he explained. 'I think they're about half a million quid at the moment. You put liquid hydrogen in it. When it runs out of hydrogen, it switches over to petrol. It's a BM V-12 engine with different injectors in it that can do hydrogen as well as petrol. I don't know if that's a dream car, but it's an interesting car.'

It was a world away from his worst car, a Ford Escort. 'It had done 40,000 miles and the engine blew up, which seemed to be par for the course with Ford Escorts at the time because they were rubbish,' he revealed.

With his family, though, he enjoyed the quiet life. 'I'm self-contained,' he admitted. 'I can amuse myself – sit and play the piano, read, write. But Gia is as well – she's learning Egyptian at the moment.' As the kids grew older, Milinovich threw herself back into work, while acknowledging, 'My current project is our children, mainly. They're brilliant projects. Very, very tiring and not a lot of thinking involved, so it's quite hard.' And she made sure her husband stayed grounded. 'Turning into a TV star is the last thing on my mind but there's no way she would let it happen,' said Cox. 'She always says she could tell any admirer some tales that would put them right off me.'

Gia became Jonathan Ross's new media advisor, helping the star out with his online ideas. 'He's writing comics at the moment, so I'm hoping to start doing more things,' she said. 'He's lovely. I'm playing it by ear. Trying to just keep the house going while Brian's away actually is a full-time job.'

Cox's continued piano practice was to serve him well after he received a phone call from an old friend. D:Ream's Peter Cunnah had been working in the record industry since breaking up the band, but in a more behind-the-scenes capacity.

However, a chance meeting during an afternoon walk brought the former chart-topper crashing into his past. He bumped into his old bandmate Al Mackenzie on a bench in a park and the pair started talking about old times. Unintentionally, the band was now back together. An album called *The Platinum Collection* containing an array of remixes and old material had been released without their input in 2006. Cunnah believed the time was right to unveil some new songs. Thus were the seeds sewn for *In Memory Of…*, a record which eventually came out in March 2011. There was one key – and independently now very famous – former band member who needed to be contacted, though.

'It took a while for us to catch up, but we finally managed to get hold of [Brian] in Chicago via satellite phone,' Cunnah told Sosogay.org. Cox was thrilled to hear from his old bandmates. 'The album's essentially finished and Pete called me up and said, "Just for old time's sake, do you want to stick a few keyboards on a couple of the songs?"' he told the BBC. 'I said, "Yeah, brilliant!" It was a great bit of my life and I just wanted to give it another go, but the last time I played with D:Ream was in 1997 at the election. I've probably forgotten how to play.'

The album was eventually released at the same time as *Wonders of the Universe* appeared on our television screens, although Cunnah described this as being a coincidence. 'He thinks there's a link between music, science and art – and he's right,' said the singer/songwriter. 'He's contributed on three tracks on the album. He's actually been issued [with] a bit of a gagging order by the BBC not to talk about us in science-y interviews – we're not cool enough!' Cox said he wouldn't be touring with the band, but the album did solid indie business and had its fans, achieving four-and-a-half stars out of five on Amazon. It wasn't enough for Cox to return to music, but has probably increased the likelihood of a Dare reunion some time in the near future.

Perhaps the greatest impact he has made as he moves forward is just how much debate there is about science in the media and how much he's influenced young people to feel involved in that debate. 'Certainly in the UK there's been a renewed interest in rational thought,' he said. 'That might seem surprising to say, as you might assume that as the centuries pass, societies become more rational but we haven't really. In the 18th century, science was the thing to do if you were important, but we've lost that.' But all that appears to be changing. A nationwide survey of 2,000 parents by the Big Bang UK Science & Engineers Fair, of which Brian Cox is a spokesman, found that a quarter of parents thought their children knew more than they did about science. Cox even offered his services to answer some of the most likely questions a parent would be asked by their offspring, including how aeroplanes stay in the air, why the sky is blue, why water is wet and how to do long division.

'The best thing parents can do is work with their children to find the answers,' he said. 'Not only can it be fun, but you'll both learn something new along the way.' He equated this newfound attitude to how the great scientific innovators worked. 'Most scientists are interested in just looking at the universe, looking at nature,' he told The A.V. Club. 'I don't think there are many great discoveries that you can point to that were the result of someone wanting to find the answer to a particular question. If you look back at Einstein or Newton, you find that people are fascinated often by the smallest things, actually. In terms of Einstein, cosmology – which is a real part of the way the universe evolved, the way the universe began, the Big Bang – all that stuff came from Einstein really just being interested in the speed of light. He was just interested; it was a question he'd always asked. He'd always wondered about how light travels. It's a useful lesson, in general, not only to the theories, but that science is at its best when curious people are just trying to find things out.'

The increasing frequency of discoveries at CERN continued to excite him. 'The big question is the origin and mass of the universe,' he insisted to Universe Today. 'It is very, very important because it is not an end in itself. It is a fundamental part of Quantum Field Theory, which is our theory of three of the four forces of nature. So, if you ask the question on the most basic level of how does the universe work, there are only two pillars of our understanding at the moment. There is Einstein's Theory of General Relativity, which deals with gravity – the weakest force in the Universe that deals with the shape of space and time, and all those things. But everything else – electromagnetism, the way the atomic nuclei works, the way molecules work, chemistry, all that – everything else is what's called a Quantum Field Theory. Embedded in that is called the Standard Model of particle physics. And embedded in that is this mechanism for generating mass and it's just so fundamental. It's not just kind of an interesting add-on, it's right [at] the heart of the way the theory works. So, understanding whether our current picture of the Universe is right – and if there is this thing called the Higgs mechanism or whether there is something else going on – is critical to our progress because it is built into that picture.

'There are hints in the data recently that maybe that mechanism is right. We have to be careful. It's not a very scientific thing to say that we have hints. We have these thresholds for scientific discovery, and we have them for a reason because you get these statistical flukes that appear in the data and when you get more data, they go away again. I think it is very important to emphasise that this is not just a lot of particle physicists looking for particles because that's their job. It is the fundamental part of our understanding of three of the four forces of nature.'

As the team appeared to ever closer to finding the elusive Higgs, he was thrilled. Speaking in August 2011, he said: 'The latest results were published in a set of conferences a few weeks ago and they are just under what is called the "Three Sigma" level. That is the way of assessing how significant the results are. The thing about all quantum theory and particle physics in general is it is all statistical. If you do *this* a thousand times, then three times *this* should happen, and eight times *that* should happen, so it's all statistics. As you know, if you toss a coin, it can come up heads ten times – there is a probability for that to happen. It doesn't mean the coin is weighted or there's something wrong with it, that's just how statistics is so there are intriguing hints that they have found something interesting.

'Both experiments at the Large Hadron Collider, the ATLAS and the Compact Muon Solenoid (CMS) recently reported "excess events," where there were more events than would be expected if the Higgs does not exist. It is about the right mass: we think the Higgs particle should be somewhere between about 120 and 150 gigaelectron volts, which is the expected mass range of the Higgs. These hints are around 140, so that's good, it's where it should be, and it is behaving in the way that it is predicted to by the theory. The theory also predicts how it should decay away, and what the probability should be, so all the data is that this is consistent with the so-called standard model Higgs. But so far, these events are not consistently significant enough to make the call.

'It is important that the Tevatron has glimpsed it as well, but that has even a lower significance because that was low energy and not as many collisions there so you've got to be scientific about things. There is a reason we have these barriers – these thresholds are to be cleared to claim discoveries and we haven't cleared it yet, but it is fascinating. It's the first time one of these rumours have been, you know, not just nonsense. It really is a genuine piece of exciting physics. But you have to be scientific about these things: it's not that we know it is there and we're just not going to announce it yet. It's the statistics aren't here yet to claim the discovery. The thing about the Higgs, it is so fundamentally embedded in quantum theory. You've got to explore it because it is one thing to see a hint of a new particle, but it's another thing to understand how that particle behaves. There are lots of different ways the Higgs particles can behave and there are lots of different mechanisms.'

At time of writing, despite a couple of false positives, Higgs still hasn't been discovered and Cox emphasised the need to keep finding new ways of investigating. 'There are a huge amount of questions,' he said. 'The Higgs theory as it is now doesn't explain why the particles have the masses they do. It doesn't explain why the top quark, which is the heaviest of the fundamental particles, is something like 180 times heavier than the proton. It's a tiny point-like thing with no size but it's 180 times the mass of a proton! That is heavier than some of the heaviest atomic nuclei! Why? We don't know.

I think it is correct to say there is a door that needs to be opened that has been closed in our understanding of the Universe for decades. It is so fundamental that we've got to open it before we can start answering these further questions, which are equally intriguing, but we need this answered first. Well, I think it will – because this is part of *the* fundamental theory of the forces of nature. So, quantum theory in the past has given us an understanding, for example, of the way semiconductors work and it underpins our understanding of modern technology and the way chemistry works, the way that biological systems work – it's all there. This is the theory that describes it all. I think having a radical shift and deepening in understanding of the basic laws of nature will change the way that physics proceeds in the 21st century without a doubt – it is *that* fundamental. So, who knows?

'At every paradigm shift in science, you never really could predict what it was going to do, but the history of science tells you that it did something quite remarkable. Some of our theories, you look at them and wonder how we worked them! The answer is mathematically, the same way that Einstein came up with General Relativity, with mathematical predictions. It is remarkable we've been able to predict something so fundamental about the way that empty space behaves. We might turn out to be right.'

When CERN appeared to have fired sub-atomic particles known as neutrinos 453.6 miles from the lab near Geneva to the Gran Sasso laboratory near Rome at a speed faster than the speed of light, it looked as though Cox would have to revise some of his core theories. He had been asked about the possibility of time travel before and always had the same answer. 'Travel into the indefinite future is absolutely possible,' he told *Metro*. 'If you flew around space close to the speed of light for about four years, you'd come back to earth 40,000 years in the future. Amazingly, Einstein predicted it in 1905.'

But there were theoretical exceptions, thanks to Uncle Albert. 'The precise thing is that in special relativity – that's Einstein's theory for space and time, not gravity– in that theory, time travel is prevented 100 per cent,' he explained. 'In his theory of gravity and general relativity, it's possibly just about permitted, but most people think that will be closed off. It's thought that it is probably a problem with our understanding of the theory. There are things called wormholes that can exist in Einstein's general theory of relativity, which are little tunnels through space and time. They are the science-fiction wormholes, essentially. Like in *Deep Space 9*. Those things are valid solutions to the theory, but most people think they'll be unstable when we get a better understanding of gravity – quantum gravity, actually. There's a tiny, tiny crack in the door where you could say, "Maybe." But I think most sensible people doubt it. Being able to go back in time and stop your parents from getting together isn't a fantastic way to run a universe anyway.'

Because of the scientific consensus of a cosmic speed limit – hitherto considered to be the speed of light – he was able to say to this. The Gran Sasso experiment potentially threw some of these comments into doubt. It was an area of science that would seek to challenge him – and cause him to receive a lot of time travel-related questions – as it progressed.

As a celebrity, however, Brian Cox is an anomaly. He's the kind of person who can talk with conviction and knowledge about astronomy and particle physics, as well as make comments such as: 'I don't want to scare anybody, but it is overwhelmingly likely that we'll get hit by a very large piece of rock from space at some point in the future – we've got to be prepared for that.' All without getting laughed at while he does so. He's famous enough to be asked whether he has ever contemplated a guest spot on *Doctor Who* and appears to have such influence that he once said: 'I read that Courtney Love and Anne Hathaway both said, about a week apart, that they were reading books about quantum physics. I think it's becoming a Hollywood badge of honour.'

He's also a celebrity described by one commentator as having 'backed into the limelight' – a humble, average guy who is now seen as the face of UK science. And it's a position that his peers are happy for him to occupy. 'I've seen him on the telly – he's got pretty good communication skills,' says Professor Paddy Regan from the University of Surrey. 'He's passionate about his science. He's as qualified as anybody else to speak about it. From everything I've seen from Brian Cox, I think it's genuinely true that he passionately cares that science is important for culture and society.' So far, he has managed to stay on the right side of the fame game, mainly through sticking to advice given by his friend and collaborator Dara O'Briain – 'We were in a bar in Soho one night and I told Brian the first rule of showbiz: What would David Attenborough do?' said O'Briain. 'Nothing with the word "celebrity" in the title, nothing involving eating kangaroo parts in the jungle and no hosting light-hearted quiz shows.' And he does it all with a smile, convincing his audience that the intricate formulae and theorems he talks about are simple to grasp.

'I don't think physics is easy,' says Professor Regan. 'It's a discipline.' Yet Cox has apparently sparked a renaissance in the topic among young people while managing to convince the right people, at least publicly, that his chosen career is one worth investing in. Science programming has always had a place on television, from Sir Patrick Moore and Carl Sagan to David Attenborough and *Tomorrow's World*, but rarely has it enjoyed such primetime status or had so many TV hosts reaching for the chemical engineering degree for which they thought they had abandoned the need the moment they took off their mortarboards. Much of this is thanks to a man who once sported a terrible mullet while playing keyboards in Oldham squash club, who sported a tartan waistcoat on *Top of the Pops*, who taught his toddler son to love rocket launches and who got a D in his mathematics A-level.

Just remember, as a Northern man, he doesn't like any kind of fuss.

CHAPTER 11
COX'S LAWS

Any scientist worth his salt has their own law. Whether it's Einstein, Newton, or the Newcastle-born physicist Peter Higgs, who in 1964 came up with the concept of the God particle (otherwise known as the Higgs boson), one of the main reasons for the creation of the Large Hadron Collider. Brian Cox once proclaimed his own law to Shortlist. 'Cox's law,' he said, 'states that the size of your audience is directly proportional to the amount of shit people talk about you.'

While this may be true when you are a famous television personality on top of being a scientist, it's not something that will be cited in academic papers for years to come. On the other hand, Cox is never, as is clear from the above statement, afraid to speak his mind and there are a number of issues to which he continually returns in almost every interview. They're his passions, his bête-noirs, the things he holds dearest and those he gets most angry about every time he sits down in front of a microphone. Herewith the Five Laws of Brian Cox.

1. Creationism is a crock

And he's not afraid to say it. Of course, it comes from a position of science, rather than a specific antipathy to the idea of faith. At least it has since he became an adult. He told the *Observer* about his early religious forays: 'I was sent to Sunday school for a few weeks, but I didn't like getting up on Sunday mornings.' His views have matured a little since then. Asked by the *Guardian* what he would do if confronted by a ghost, he answered: 'It's my view that the existence of ghosts would contravene the second law of thermodynamics. The principle of the conservation of energy and the fact that entropy always increases, you'd be hard put to throw that away. You'd have to rip the book up – that's what it would imply if you saw a ghost. I would say, "I could not be more surprised than I am by the fact that thermodynamics appears to be shit."' In a vodcast with fellow TV presenter Robert Llewellyn, he was asked a similar question, about whether he could countenance the afterlife. The answer? A convoluted explanation about the heaters on the back of fridges and how if he ended up in heaven, he would be confused as to how a fridge manages to work. So, what is the second law of thermodynamics? The first law, better known as the Law of Conservation of Matter, basically means matter and/or energy cannot be destroyed. The amount of it within the universe remains the same.

The second law is otherwise called the Law of Increased Entropy. This means that as energy is used productively (for example, in keeping a human alive), it is turned into unusable energy. As such, the usable energy is lost forever. Physicists would then conclude that since no more energy is created and more and more is being turned into something unusable, *nothing* is eternal. Which means, in some people's opinions including Brian Cox, there is no God and no afterlife.

He has displayed his anger towards those who believe the world will end in 2012, calling anyone who thinks this a 'moron'. 'We're going to do some shows, by the way, end-of-the-world shows on December 21st in 2012,' he says. 'It's going to be great – in London. We're going to do another one on the 22nd to give a refund in case we're wrong and the world ends. We're going to do a full-ticket refund on the 22nd. I thought, it's ridiculous – the world isn't going to end. But then I thought, actually, for the people who believe that the world is likely to end more quickly because they'll probably just get hit by a bus. Because they're such *idiots*, they are probably unable to effectively cross a road, so I think there is some kind of truth in it. If you really believe that stuff, you're probably going to go anyway – staring at the sky, waiting for the big hand to come down.'

But interestingly, he's not entirely dismissive of those who do have faith – unless they happen to be fundamentalists. 'You got to be blunt,' he says. 'I'm not saying religious people are full of shit, but if you believe the earth is six-and-a-half thousand years old, then you are.' He argues while he finds a militant atheist like Richard Dawkins 'very funny', he doesn't think it's the way to go about convincing people to change their belief system. 'I think creationism should be taught in science classes,' he says, 'because it's legitimate to say, "I think the earth was formed six-and-a-half thousand years ago." Then you can go, "How do you know that it wasn't?"

'We know, for example, about the Grand Canyon: we know that rivers erode, we can look at it knowing how deep it is and we can work out how old it is, and it's older than that. There are many other things, too but that's good because it tells you how to be a scientist – that's what science is. So, I have no problem with people putting forward theories about how the universe began because that's what you do: you guess and then you go and test it. You keep going, and you keep finding out you're not wrong knowing what you know, and you carry on. And eventually you get to a point where you were wrong and you replace it with something else.'

In fact, he's keen to argue that while many people try and create a schism between religion and science, he has encountered a different mindset from his ecclesiastical colleagues. After meeting on a panel about atheism, he became friends with the Dean of Guildford Cathedral and following the success of *Wonders of the Solar System*, he received an invitation to the Archbishop of Canterbury's house, who happens to be a fan of the show. 'Rowan Williams is a very thoughtful man,' Cox has said. 'If you want to move society forward in a more rational direction, religious leaders can be useful because they share that view. Setting yourself up as anti-religion is not helpful. You can set yourself up as anti-maniac, that's different. Setting yourself up as an atheist who is against all religion is not a battle that needs to be fought.' However, that doesn't mean he is prepared to alter his opinion – unless a new law of thermodynamics can be discovered. Instead, he believes we should turn to scientific solutions for our answers and be able to accept uncertainty in the same way as scientists do.

'Science to me is just the application of common sense. What you have to do is accept what you don't know. You have to draw a line and say, "Here's what I know and here's what I don't know, and how will I get there? If I want to find out this stuff, what should I do?"' But while he's keen to turn away from the idea that there is something bigger than us, that there may be things we can never understand and it might be because there is something bigger than the universe, it's ironic that Cox actually revels in the things he doesn't know. Whether this is an attitude genuinely shared by his colleagues or just Cox himself is hard to confirm but it's clear the sense of doubt, the desire to be constantly proved wrong does, somewhat bizarrely, drive at the heart of his quest for knowledge.

'The best thing a scientist can be is completely devoid of dogmatic belief,' he told Discovery.com. 'That's what I have – nothing I cling on to as a sacred view of the world. Science is the process of going to the edge of your understanding, that's a character trait I have. The ability to say "I don't know that" and then not be scared about that. I get asked when I go to talks in schools, "Well, how did the universe begin?" and I say, "I dunno" and it gets a laugh. And I say, "Don't laugh, that's actually the scientific answer. Don't know, but I've got some ideas to go and try to find out."'

This crunching of data, even on such ambiguous issues, is where Cox feels comfortable. And it could be construed as a different kind of fanaticism: one borne through solid facts.

'Religion and science come from the same position, in a way,' he says. 'They originated in people who were interested in nature and fascinated, and wanted to ask some questions about how the world works. Why are we here? How did we get here? I think it's important to recognise that there are three types of people and I have time for two of them. There's people who notice the world is beautiful and interesting, and worth explaining. That can engender a sort of religious feeling in some people. There's other people who notice that as well and it engenders a scientific feeling, which is to go explore it and use the scientific method to understand it better. And then the people I don't have much time for are the people who haven't noticed anything. If you don't notice there's something interesting at all, to me, that's the worst possible position.

'I don't have any issue pointing out that religions had had a positive effect on civilisation. Obviously they have. The feelings they are designed to play off are the same feelings that scientists have. The world is very interesting, so you want to find out how it works; that is a common feeling.' Yet while others search for an answer as to why we're here, Cox is focused on *how*. He's doing that in his work at CERN, but as he explains, 'The difference is that in a religious person's head, you tend to say "I'm not happy here, I don't like this, I don't know what happened at the Big Bang". I'm happy to say from a billionth of a second after the Big Bang, we pretty much know what happened. Less than a billionth we're not doing so well. I don't know it, and I'll gladly go and try to find out. Or you can invent something and say it was God. Then you've stopped, because you "know" what happened. Why would you do that?'

He's not worried that his beliefs and the way he presents his television programmes might offend either – even in places like America, where there are more extreme levels of evangelical Christian belief. 'I don't make the [*Wonders of the Universe*] in order to get the biggest possible audience. That's not why I do it,' he says. 'We just want to make good programmes. The moment you start trying to triangulate off people and try to follow the path of least sense – especially in a science programme – you're just lost straightaway. There's nothing I can do about it. The universe is 13.73 billion years old. When you make a programme that is about the beginning of the universe, you're going to have to say that it was 13.73 billion years ago. There's not a lot you can do about that, really. There are more scientific people in the US than there are in Britain because there are more people. So, there are more religious extremists in the US too, but that's just because there are five times as many people living in the country. What can I say? Those people are not going to watch my shows anyway.'

'Sagan wrote a very famous essay called *Religion and Science: An Alliance*, where he pointed out that really what you want in the world is a coalition of people of goodwill to move things forward,' he told writer Gregg LaGambina. 'He was thinking at the time about nuclear disarmament because in the '70s that was the great threat. Now, you've got threats to the climate; you've got threats with conflicts, which are in part driven by clashes in civilisations and clashes of extremist religions so I think you can be quite pragmatic about it and say, "Even if I thought it was a good idea, I'm not going to convince everybody in the world that they should give up religion." It's not going to happen.' He continues: 'I've pointed to some writing by St Augustine, a venerated Christian theologian from many years ago. He pointed out that once you begin to read the Bible literally then you open it to ridicule and ultimately, that's the path to the downfall of the religion. It is – because it's not a textbook. St Augustine knew that. It's not as if this is new thinking, it is a statement of the obvious.'

2. We should be doing more space exploration

Why? Because we need to prepare for when that asteroid hits. 'We've already started,' he told The A.V. Club. 'There have been humans off earth now for over a decade on the International Space Station. We're vulnerable on earth. Carl Sagan always said, "If the dinosaurs had a space program, they'd still be around."' And as someone who grew up thinking the moon landings were the most significant piece of scientific progress in history, Cox considers the future of space travel. He told BBC Slink: 'In ten years' time, you could probably get married in space. You'll be able to fly on commercial flights, weightless flights into space. Possibly not into orbit, but certainly these weightless hops that people like Virgin are going to do. In ten years, you'll be able to do that and I suspect people will be able to get married on them. Around the earth, not on the moon or anything like that, but in space.'

It won't be Cox, though he is thought to have signed up to a place on one of the first Virgin Galactic flights, due to offer passengers an astronaut-esque experience. And it's all very well pushing forward with space tourism, but Cox believes searching to definitively discover if we are alone in the universe is the one area where the scientific community is really falling behind. Don't call him a UFO-ologist, though – this is just microbial life. 'I'm sure it won't be much bigger than a microbe,' he says. 'We found an ocean on Europa, which is a moon of Jupiter that probably has twice as much water than the earth underneath the surface. It's salt water, it's incredible – bigger than the oceans of earth. In the last show of [the *Wonders of the Solar System* series], I go two kilometres down under the ocean in a submarine to see these geo-thermal vents. And there's little crabs running around there. We know from the earth that you don't need the sun – life exists anywhere there's liquid water. And we've found it on Europa. We found it on one of the moons of Saturn; we've almost certainly found it on Mars. We've found ice, but we think there's probably liquid beneath the surface. There's methane on Mars, which is seasonal. With the seasons you get more or less methane in the atmosphere and the only way you can do that on earth is by life or by geological processes. But Mars is geologically dead, we think. It's exciting, actually. *Very* exciting.'

He remains perturbed by NASA – and the UK's – lack of ambition in manned space exploration, arguing while NASA wanted to push on to Mars, small-mindedness and a misunderstanding of the scale of investment meant plans were stalled. 'Britain on its own could have gone to look for life in the three most likely places that it might exist outside the earth for the cost of bailing out the banks,' he says, astonished. 'That should make you think. It sounds ridiculous and it's a silly political thing because obviously we had to bail out the banks, but it still sets the scale. It's overwhelmingly important to go to these places.

'The last episode is about life and is called *Aliens*. To go and search for life beneath the surface of other worlds is for me the most important question we could try to address. It's one of the few great questions we could answer. We actually know how to possibly find the answer to say definitively we're not alone in the universe; we know how to do that, we know the places to look. And the fact we don't do it, when it's astonishingly cheap.'

It's clear that he has taken his cue from his hero Carl Sagan, who more than 30 years ago was doing his best to convince civilians about the sums involved in space exploration in a similar way to how Cox is doing now. 'The budget for space sciences in the United States is enormous. Comparable expenditures in the Soviet Union are a few times larger,' Sagan wrote in his 1980 book, *Cosmos*. Sagan goes even further than Cox, suggesting serious manned space flight will never occur until the countries of the world undertake a dramatic stance on nuclear, as well as conventional disarmament.

Cox doesn't advocate this, but he does point to exploration for exploration's sake as being crucial to the future of the human race. 'There's a very famous quote from [Alexander] Fleming, when he discovered penicillin. He said something like, "On September something 1928, I didn't expect to wake up and revolutionise medicine,"' he says. 'He woke up playing around with little bits of mould in his kitchen, basically – he was just interested in mouldy things. And he revolutionised everybody's life. *Everybody*. Virtually everybody who is over the age of about 40 and 50 is alive today because of antibiotics. Virtually everybody would have died, if it hadn't been for that. And it wasn't someone trying to discover antibiotics that did it – it was someone exploring nature. So, the argument, "Couldn't we just spend our money making everybody's lives better?" We *are* doing that. That's what exploration actually does.'

It's not hard to see why he was so buoyed by the news in early December 2011 of a new earth-like planet discovered by CERN scientists. Kepler 22-B is thought to have a temperature of 22°C, is 2.4 times the size of earth and 600 light years away. 'Beyond the Solar System, the search for exoplanets is going very, very well,' says Cox. 'Virtually every star we survey, we find planets! Well, that might be a bit of an exaggeration, but we've found hundreds and hundreds of planets.' It's not yet known what the basic essence of the newly-found planet is, but as Cox told interviewer Richard Bacon: 'You've got [a] planet there for the first time in the right place around a star to have oceans of water on the surface possibly. If we're not alone, that probably means there's a universe teeming with life.' He may not know whether there are other kinds of life in the universe and whether space exploration would ever get us there, but he echoes Sagan again in suggesting that it's crucial we find out. 'Imagine if there's one civilisation,' he says, 'how valuable does that make us? Would it make us behave rather differently?'

3. Repeat: increasing science funding and getting kids in schools to continue studying science is key to our world prospering in the future. Science is part of everything.

This is Cox's version of a unified theory. It's imperative that the world realises how fundamental science is to budgets, our children, to everything – and the requisite people should alter their mindset immediately. He complained to the *Daily Telegraph*: 'It's still acceptable in this country for people to say, while drinking their claret, "Of course, I don't understand science – I did classics." Everyone will laugh, but saying you don't know anything about science at all should be like driving around without a seatbelt or something. It should become an unacceptable thing to do.' As such, Cox tirelessly campaigns for increased government funding and improved education, and he's not afraid to admit his agenda.

'I want to use the platform I have to put pressure on the Government and on decision-makers to support science. I'm completely open about that,' he says. That means tracking down Minister of State for Universities and Science David Willetts at the 2010 Conservative Party Conference to ensure he got the message about funding and speaking at pre-election events such as Eureka Live, which examined some of the key issues at stake in science. 'I'll say it to [David] Cameron, if I get to him,' he told the *Daily Mail*, 'make Britain the best place in the world to do science and engineering. It's a realistic ambition.' With a figure of 6.7 per cent of Britain's gross domestic product (GDP) said to come from physics-based industries, Cox was frustrated at the powers-that-be and in his eyes, their failure to expand science funding. 'We've got so little money that we only fund things like CERN and the European Space Agency, which are absolutely excellent and bound to work,' he said. 'Any venture capitalist will tell you that you don't just want to fund things that are guaranteed to work.'

And Cox was not afraid to stand up in defiance against the head of the main physics funding body when a report by MPs criticised the way Professor Keith Mason handled an £80 million hole in his body's budget. Mason was chief executive of the Science and Technology Facilities Council (STFC) and came under fire in April 2008 before a parliamentary committee. The report stated his decision-making 'raises serious questions about the role and performance of the chief executive, especially his ability to retain the confidence of the scientific community, as well as carry through the necessary changes.' Unafraid to stand up against the status quo, Cox, as a member of the UK Particle Physics Action Group, said: 'If it was my organisation and I read that, I would resign. The organisation needs new management at the top.' As it was, Mason stayed until late 2011, but the episode demonstrated Cox's passion for ensuring science – and the money given to it – was treated with respect.

Those in the scientific community, including Cox, worried that the budgetary crisis would lead to Britain having to pull out of important international physics projects, threatened the work of the Jodrell Bank Observatory and would scale back the number of experiments running on the Large Hadron Collider at CERN.

Two years later, in early 2010, Cox was railing just as hard in a no-holds-barred, two-pronged attack in the *New Scientist* on the monetary crisis with the STFC. He argued that the funding issues had been carrying on for longer than many people realised – since 2007, when the STFC received the lowest increase in useable cash from the British government of all research councils other than Arts and Humanities. And he suggested the subsequent cuts and reprioritisation within the scientific community when it came to British endeavours and participation was a direct result of the initial low monetary injection.

Cox directly blames the Labour government for their part in what he sees as a disaster and says in the article that it should be considered an election issue (Labour, of course, lost the election). He also targets top dogs in the comparatively new STFC (an amalgamation of two smaller bodies) after a select committee report reported: 'The timing of the formation of the STFC was not propitious. It takes time to set up a new organisation, especially one as large and complex as STFC. The government's expectation that STFC would be ready for a new Comprehensive Spending Review (CSR) was overly ambitious.' Cox ripostes: 'It raises very serious questions about the role of STFC's senior management and their ability to communicate with top civil servants.'

It's worth noting that the *New Scientist* article came out before Cox's show, *Wonders of the Solar System*, hit the air. With his subsequent increase in fame (and the change in government), he has found himself with closer access to the decision-makers, a fact he lamented somewhat in a radio interview when he mentioned those on television do seem more likely to gain direct contact with those who matter. In 2010, he wrote: 'Despite a hell of a lot of digging, I don't know who to question about the origins of the STFC crisis.' What stuck in his craw and continues to do so is what he potentially perceives as negative attitudes towards science within the corridors of power. Cox argues that the 2007 spending cuts, which were carefully presented to avoid seeming like direct cuts, make it seem as if there's a 'deep malaise in our country.' Indeed, he charged his fellow scientists to stand up against the funding backlash – 'We must stand together, put aside interdisciplinary in-fighting and raise the volume of our voices in the public arena.' While his tone may appear to be more temperate as his fame grows, it's safe to say the fight hasn't gone out of him.

He considered it a personal triumph when Chancellor of the Exchequer George Osborne froze spending on science despite other austerity measures in October 2010, but was particularly vociferous about the way the coalition government had upped tuition fees for universities, telling interviewer Cole Moreton: 'If you get to a point where you are discouraging people who haven't got a lot of money from going to university, then first of all it's immoral. Second, it's ludicrous to think that if there is an Einstein or a Newton out there, then they are going to come from a rich family.'

It's understandable that the cuts touched a nerve since Cox is first and foremost an academic researcher and a professor at Manchester University, and has spent a vast amount of his working life in a university-funded laboratory. 'It is a very dangerous game because I don't think it is understood what effect it will have on the behaviour of young people,' he has said. 'What government is about is building the foundation to the future of the country and it's a pre-requisite for the future success of Britain that we are a scientific country.' It's possible, too that he feels – like many prosperous people of his age, especially those already working within research fields – a pang of guilt at his own free ride through the university system.

Perhaps that's why he is so gung-ho in his work with schools.

Each week, he receives dozens of requests to speak at schools, almost all of which his schedule will not allow. However, he does work with events such as the annual The Big Bang: UK Young Scientists & Engineers Fair, which bids to celebrate and raise the profile of young people's achievements in science and engineering, as well as to enable more youngsters to experience the excitement and opportunities through science. 'People – especially kids – have the idea that you need to be a genius if you want to gain access to the scientific world,' he told interviewer Danny Scott. 'That's not true. If science, technology or engineering capture your imagination, then stick with them. The opportunities are there. The average 15-year-old probably dreams of winning *The X Factor* or playing for Manchester United. That's only going to happen to a tiny number of people, but society is crying out for scientists. And if you do choose the profession, the possibilities are literally endless. They stretch far beyond the pop music chart – as far as your imagination. You might change the way we view life itself!'

In November 2010, Springfield School in the Portsmouth suburb of Drayton won a competition to receive a one-off lesson from Professor Brian Cox, thanks to the fair and he was left overwhelmed by the response he received. In January 2012, it was the turn of Morley Academy in Leeds (who won the second incarnation of the same competition). Dubbing it 'my lesson of a lifetime', the lucky students went to Manchester University's Jodrell Bank Observatory, where they got a chance to see the famous Lovell Telescope. 'We're always looking at ways of inspiring our pupils to love science – but this is something else!' Morley head teacher John Townsley told the

Huffington Post UK: 'I'm sure some of the students involved will look back on this trip as the inspiration they needed to follow their dreams and pursue a successful career in science and engineering.' Speaking to the *Yorkshire Evening Post*, student Rosie Hassan said: 'I did not think the day would be as interesting as it turned out to be. It was an invaluable experience, one I will never forget. Brian Cox is a fantastic ambassador for physics: he is engaging and inspiring, he has a great ability to connect with his audience.' Fellow pupil Tina Wearing added: 'Brian Cox is a legend! It was very engaging and I want to watch more of him.'

One of his and Manchester University's physics department's philosophies is to open up young people's minds to the breadth of jobs available to science graduates. 'I think science has got to be cool for kids,' said Cox, looking back on his own immediate and unquenchable passion for the topic. 'In a few years' time you could be building a Mars rover, a F1 car or designing special effects for *Lord of the Rings*.' He's quick to point out to ambivalent teens that their iPod works because of quantum mechanics, or that the internet on which they surf 24 hours a day was invented at CERN by Tim Berners-Lee. Luckily, his skill in conveying his passion for the subject, as well as his undoubted fame, generally means young people listen.

'I find it remarkable that you can get an auditorium full of students essentially just listening about particle physics and cosmology,' he told the *Manchester Evening News*. 'That's very gratifying.' He adds: 'I want to use the platform I have to put pressure on the government and on decision-makers to support science. I'm completely open about that.'

4. Climate change is real – and those who disagree are 'irritating'

'Climate modelling is difficult science, but there is a consensus about the modelling,' says Cox. He argues scientists are not telling people what to do, not forcing them to rid themselves of their SUVs, merely telling them what is true. During his 2010 Huw Wheldon Lecture, in which he discussed science on television, he even praised the controversial climate change-denier documentary by Martin Durkin, a programme lauded by deniers and vilified by believers. While calling it 'factually total bollocks', he suggested it raised good questions about the politicisation of science, although he preferred to call it a polemic rather than a documentary. 'Even though I don't agree with the point of view expressed in the film, I would defend the right of the filmmaker absolutely to express an opinion,' he explained to his audience.

Nonetheless, he is firm on the science and intractable in his own view. 'We know that if you put CO_2 into the atmosphere, it warms the earth up,' he says. 'That's true. So then you may be able to have a debate about how much, [but] it's very difficult to work these things out because our computer models are not very good. So it's pretty likely that it's not due to an increase in solar output, although the sun decreases and increases its output and we don't know why. But with global warming you can see the mechanism and once you know the mechanism, you can accept that it's true. Then you can start arguing.'

Suggesting it's a good way to teach science in schools – building models, taking data, testing the data, getting a result – Cox is vociferous in rooting his theories in background detail, especially from those who might claim the earth has an ability to self-heal, thus negating the need for climate change debate. He's not afraid to posit ideas which offer deniers a lifeline, while simultaneously and subtly slamming the door in their face. 'The thing is that life seems to find a way to inhabit any corner of the universe that it physically can,' he says. 'As an example, the sun was 25 per cent less bright 3 billion years ago. From our models of how stars evolve, we can predict the brightness. I think it's because of the explanation "what the hell happened then?" because it should have been frozen, if you think about it.

'Actually, we know that the atmosphere in the earth was very carbon dioxide-rich because there were no plants and plants take carbon dioxide out of the atmosphere. So there was an intense Greenhouse Effect, which allowed the earth to be hot enough for liquid water to exist and life to develop. We know there was lots of carbon dioxide in the atmosphere, we know that all our models of stars say they start off less bright and grow brighter and then die – it's through a combination of models that we know that. So the Greenhouse Effect was very fortunate at that point because it allowed life to begin. And then as life took CO_2 out of the atmosphere, the sun got brighter. It just tells you how precarious the balance is.'

'It's a nasty issue in the UK,' he told The A.V. Club, 'but certainly in the US because all that science does is tell you the most likely thing that will happen, given the available data of our understanding of the climate. Given the data we've got and the understanding we've got, then we're committed to a temperature rise. At the upper end of the predictions, it's catastrophic. It's absolute disaster. If you're looking at a four-degree temperature rise by the end of the century, then we're in *deep shit*! But if you look at the lower end, it is perhaps manageable. The reason there's a big range of predictions is because it is difficult – that's the non-political thing to say. You can't argue with that, because that's the science. The science is the science – it's there. Here's the data, here's the understanding; there it is. The policy comes in with the question of, "What do you do with that information?" You can take the view that you do nothing. You could say, "I think the markets will deal with it – insurance premiums will go up." Or, you could take a more active role and you increase things and put green taxes on things, so I can see where the political debate comes from.

'The problem with the issue is that it's turned into an attack on science on some level. That's ridiculous. The science is what the science is, and it is completely apolitical. It's a problematic issue, it's an issue that will have to have a political solution, but all that scientists can do is tell you what the current level of understanding is. If you don't think the Greenhouse Effect is a problem, then you should be sent to Venus; that would be the only useful thing to do. Send a spacecraft to Venus full of all the people who don't think the Greenhouse Effect is a problem. That'd be fun. Get rid of 'em – they'd melt. Quickly.'

5. Tweet as if your life depends on it

At the time of writing, Professor Brian Cox has 584,598 followers on Twitter and has tweeted more than 6,000 times. But that's not a patch on his wife Gia, an early proponent of the 140-character form as a new media expert, who has tweeted more than 24,000 times, though she's miles behind her husband in terms of followers with just over 14,000. The small group of people Cox follows are an interesting mix of celebrities – Phillip Schofield and Richard Bacon – and well-known academics such as maths writer Alex Bellos and TV physicist Jim Al-Khalili.

Being apart so much obviously meant online communication became an invaluable tool for Gia and Brian, as well as an opportunity for him to reply to questions about where he was. 'Sadly I missed myself on #QI,' he wrote in October 2011, 'because (honestly) I'm having breakfast next to a volcano in the Philippines filming proton gradients.' But Cox admitted his wife didn't only use it to get in touch with him while he was wandering through a desert. 'Gia uses Twitter to tell me to stop watching TV and come to bed,' he joked.

He kept his profile up to date incrementally, keeping his ongoing project as 'working on a book and lecture course at the University of Manchester' while changing whatever he was filming at the time. Gia's was simpler, reading: 'Comedy lover. Science groupie. Professional dork'. Being an open source social network, though, meant Cox and Milinovich's own views were not the only ones perpetuated in cyberspace. Shortlist set up a hashtag called #briancoxknowseverything and Cox didn't realise they were the instigators when he mentioned how much he loved the tag to them during an interview. 'Everyone thinks I know everything now,' he said. 'There's even a hashtag on Twitter called #briancoxknowseverything, where people suggest the most ludicrous, unknowable things that I may have the answer to. I loved it. My favourite response was "Brian Cox knows what Willis is talkin' 'bout."'

That *Diff'rent Strokes* reference was not the only silly Tweet in the strand. Emulating the popular Chuck Norris meme where people suggested things that showed off Norris's hard man image to ridiculous extremes, Tweeters revelled in creating feats that Cox had either accomplished or could do. @sp3ccylad Tweeted: 'Brian Cox has Shergar's address and writes to him regularly: in Horse,' while @calamitykate suggested: 'Professor Brian Cox knows where Wally is without even looking.' @squigmig focused on his scientific nature, writing: 'Professor Brian Cox knows it's not butter and has an equation to prove it.'

The hero worship-cum-mickey-taking continued with more than one an entire Twitter handle, run anonymously but Tweeting as @ProfBrianCocks and @Prof_BrianCocks (there's a theme here). The former ran out of steam pretty quickly, writing 59 entries as a man described as 'keyboardist for The Universe', with the comedy set-up that he shares a house with Sir Patrick Moore and astrologer Russell Grant. Pretending to chart the internal feuds going on between the three men as housemates, one Tweet said: 'I hate them both but I don't get paid enough to move out. I can only afford this place because of the old music royalties.'

@Prof_BrianCocks was a bit more of a professional lampooning. With more than 3,000 followers, the writer established his parody intentions up front, dubbing himself the 'Sex Science Dude' and writing some more philosophical, yet equally crazy entries, as well as flat-out gags. 'Producers of #bbcstargazing axed segment where Dara and I tell the story of the Universe's birth through interpretive dance,' read one, while another added: 'Please note that there will not be an online Q&A after #bbcstargazing as Wikipedia is down.' Comedy aside however, Twitter was something Cox took to with verve, even if he had to deal with abuse from those who didn't agree with his vociferous views about the Mayan Apocalypse and supermoons crashing into earth. In fact, his unyielding refusal to temper his retorts to those who propagated what he believed to be stupidity set him apart from many other celebrity Tweeters, who used the site more as an advertising tool than anything else.

His inability to keep quiet in the face of unbending adherence to non-scientific beliefs has already been documented here but in a sphere where many famous folk have come unstuck with what may have seemed like an offhand remark at the time, Cox was admirably honest. And in the process he may well have become the country's primary user of the word 'nobber'. His continuing belief that he was merely a university academic who had taken some time out to do a little bit of telly showed itself in the way he interacted with his hundreds of thousands of Twitter devotees. As did his clear desire to pursue an ongoing dialogue with his audience, whose online questions he sometimes answered. 'For those that asked,' he wrote, 'the origin of low entropy in the universe at the Big Bang is probably THE biggest mystery in cosmology.'

As his celebrity increases even more, it will be interesting to see how much that changes. What won't change is the closest he gets to advertising on his feed – pushing science into the public consciousness. That's either in linking to his favourite article about scientific research, or penning something such as: 'Science is a framework designed to remove the effects of human prejudice'. With so many people hanging on his every word, it's possible he might just convince them.